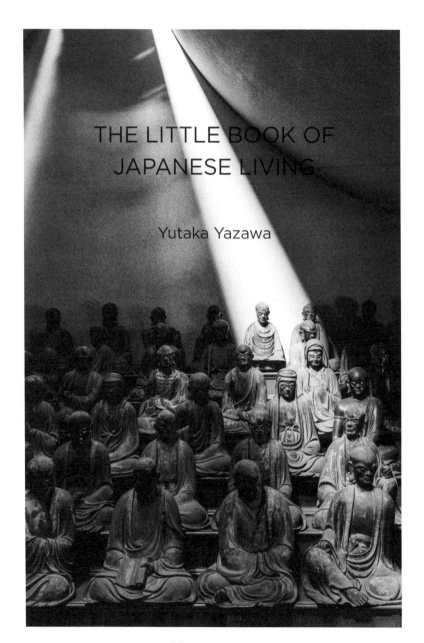

THE LITTLE BOOK OF JAPANESE LIVING

Yutaka Yazawa

WHITE LION PUBLISHING

Introduction

Tokyo is an overwhelming place, even for the Japanese. The city itself contains over 13 million people. The commuter region immediately around it is home to almost 44 million. In the era of megacities, Tokyo is the biggest of all. When I come home to Tokyo from overseas, what always strikes me is that nearly all the people are Japanese. It may sound obvious, but the level of diversity one gets accustomed to in other major cities of the world – ethnically, culturally, aesthetically – is comparatively absent in Tokyo. There is a sense of claustrophobia on a grand scale. And that is the first paradox you encounter in Japan. What appears to be the same can be very different in millions of not so obvious ways. Here, diversity is deep, if subtle.

Of course, Tokyo is only one part of Japan. Over 70 per cent of the country is mountainous, and two-thirds is covered by forest. Nature also makes its presence known through periodic typhoons and earthquakes. The world-famous Shinkansen bullet train shoots across the front of Mount Fuji, one of the many volcanoes which are actively dormant. Despite having some of the world's most advanced technology, for the Japanese, their environment instils both fear and reverence.

I was born in 1970 on the outskirts of Tokyo, and brought up there until I was 19 years old. As a result, I am naturally partial to Tokyo's ways, as opposed to life in the countryside. You may sense elements of superiority in my way of describing the provinces, cities and towns outside Tokyo. You might also feel that I am overcritical in relation to some aspects of Japanese society. I have two answers to that. Firstly, make no mistake: I love my country. However, as Malcolm X said, you should not be so blind with patriotism that you cannot face reality. I have tried to be honest to my own values and sensibilities. In that sense, this is truly personal.

Secondly, I believe that modern Japanese people are, by nature, self-critical. Our country, closed to foreigners, had been ruled by the samurai, who were supposed to be superhumanly brave and strong. But they did not stand a chance against the Europeans, and later on, Americans who forced Japan open. In the shadow of western imperialism, we asked ourselves if we had become 'good enough' to stand on our own.

You may find other partiality of which I am not as aware as those mentioned above. I thank you in advance for accepting them as my personal shortcomings, and hope that you find what follows nevertheless informative.

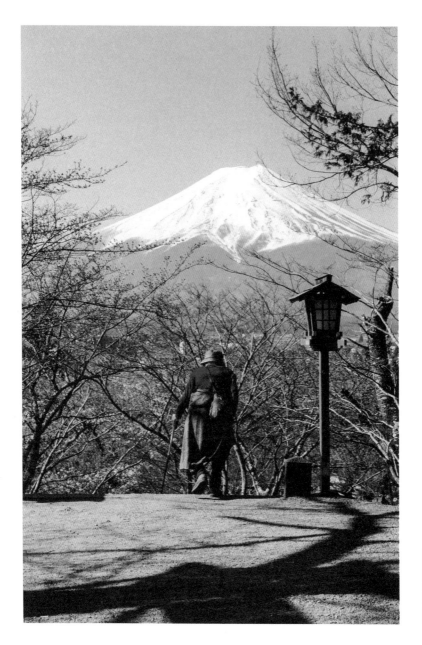

Areas of Japan

Okinawa region
沖縄地方

Chūgoku · Shikoku
regions
中国・四国地方

Ho
re
北陸

Kyūshū
region

九州地方

KYOTO

●大
OSA

近畿地方
Kinki region

Hokkaido region
北海道

Kōshin'etsu region
甲信越地方

東北地方
Tōhoku region

TOKYO
●東京

関東地方
Kantō region

地方
region

Kantō 関東地方

Kantō is the area around Tokyo (東京), made up of seven prefectures: Tokyo, Kanagawa, Chiba, Saitama, Gunma, Tochigi and Ibaraki. From the old capital of Kyoto, it was the eastern frontier land, with the name 'Kantō' meaning 'east of the gate'. It was also sometimes called 'Bandō', meaning 'east of the slope', as travellers from Kyoto saw the huge marshy plain emerging in front of them as they descended from the central mountainous region.

The samurai thrived in Kantō. When the first shogunate government was established in the 12th century, it chose the city of Kamakura, in present-day Kanagawa prefecture, as its capital. Thus started an age-long rivalry between east and west in Japan. In response to Kantō or Bandō, people gave the name 'Kansai' (関西地方) to the area around Kyoto (and later Osaka), meaning 'west of the gate'. To this day, the difference in culture and dialects between the two areas are often highlighted, rather than ignored. Even in the highly homogenised Japanese society of today, Kansai people tend to stick to their native accents when speaking among themselves.

I am Kantō-born, and spent little time outside the region until adulthood. I married a woman from Kansai, and must admit that I panicked a little when I first heard her speaking with her friends from Kansai in their native accents.

The differences extend to food. Sushi, tempura and soba noodles originated from Edo, and are regarded as Kantō foods. Kansai people say that Kantō foods are too salty, while Kantō people complain that Kansai foods are bland.

Kyoto 京都

When a city has been the capital for a millennium, even with inevitable ups and downs along the way, it cannot help but grow a character. Kyoto is definitely a character.

Kyoto, or Heian-kyō as it was called at the time, was established as a capital city in 794 by Emperor Kanmu, who wanted to break free from the established courtiers and religious powers based around the ancient capital of Nara (奈良). The deciding factor for the choice of real estate was the Chinese art of feng shui, which advised that a city must have mountains to the north, a river to the east, a lake to the south and major roads to the west. In reality, the main factor was the abundant supply of fresh water provided by the mountains surrounding Kyoto to the north, east and west. One of Kyoto's major tourist attractions to this day is the majestic Kiyomizu-dera (清水寺), a temple perched on the cliff to the east of the city. Kiyomizu literally means 'fresh water'.

As the seat of central government and the emperor, Kyoto saw many wars and conflicts. It was also a commercial centre while most of Japan remained agricultural. As a result, Kyoto people have gained a reputation for siding with the powerful and changing sides for the purpose of their own survival. They are also said to be status conscious, never speaking their own minds and the masters of condescension.

Without their conservative values and cunning, however, we would have lost Kyoto's old-fashioned charm. It's more than just ancient architecture – it is the city's entire atmosphere. The people of Kyoto have protected it against relentless and violent winds of change brought from outside. We owe much to, and have a lot to thank for, Kyoto's 'character'.

Osaka 大阪

Osaka is located at the end of Seto Naikai (瀬戸内海), Japan's extensive inland sea, at the mouth of a river that connects it to Kyoto. It became a major city in the 15th century with the building of an important temple for Jōdo Buddhism, or Pure Land Buddhism. The temple flourished not only with the devotion of its followers, but also with the improvements it provided to the city and its port facilities.

During the Tokugawa shogunate between the 17th and 19th centuries, Osaka came under its direct control and developed into a commercial hub. As feudal lords known as daimyō (大名) levied taxes on rice production, a large part of Japan's rice harvest found its way to Osaka to be converted into currency. Each feudal lord kept warehouses in Osaka, so local merchants flourished from the trade. Whilst the shogun ruled over Japan from Edo, Osaka's merchants dominated the marketplace and held the purse strings of the samurai.

The Tokugawa shogunate fell with the Meiji Restoration of 1868, but Osaka continued to thrive. Its commercial tradition meant it transitioned smoothly into modern capitalism, and the city attracted investment. Osaka was the first city to open department stores connected to train stations, a trend that would spread across Japan, and railway barons such as Ichizō Kobayashi (小林一三 1873–1957) connected the city centre with newly developed suburban residential areas. Kobayashi also developed a hot spring resort at the end of his railway line in Takarazuka (宝塚), and to attract even more visitors, he established an all-female theatre troupe called the Takarazuka Revue, which continues to be popular today.

In an homogenised Japan, Osakans proudly speak with their own dialects – which have also become the language of the entertainment business, as Osaka was the birthplace of *manzai* (漫才), a form of conversational stand-up comedy which became sensationally popular in the 1980s.

Today, Osaka is losing ground in the ongoing economic competition with Tokyo. Many corporations previously based in Osaka have moved their headquarters to Tokyo, and for some time Osaka has had to settle for being second-best. Regardless, the city retains its culture and identity, and Japan counts on Osakans to keep things real by deflating the official lines coming out of Tokyo – continuing the tradition of those powerful merchants who kept the samurai on a leash.

Tokyo 東京

Called Edo until the Meiji Restoration in 1868, Tokyo is a relatively new Japanese city. If you take a bus or taxi around Tokyo, you can see that it is built on an area that consisted of marshy swamps at the mouths of several major rivers that formed the plains of the Kantō region and flowed into Tokyo Bay. Many of the city's thoroughfares are built on covered-up small waterways and rivers which served as canals in the old days.

Edo started life in a similar way to Rome or Washington DC – its existence as a city relied solely on the fact that it was the seat of government, in this case the Tokugawa shogunate that existed between the 17th and 19th centuries.

The city is believed to have reached a population of 1 million by the beginning of the 18th century, but its rapid expansion was periodically halted by natural disasters. In addition, the initial lack of proper city planning made it vulnerable to great fires. To cap it all, earthquakes were (and, of course, still are) a major concern. In any event the native residents, known as *Edokko*, shrugged off the worries and chose to live in hope, rather than fear.

Edo's future seemed finished when the shogunate fell in the Meiji Restoration of 1868. However, the Meiji Emperor and his advisers decided to move the emperor's seat from Kyoto to Edo, whilst also changing Edo's name to Tokyo, which means 'eastern capital'. The people of Kyoto are terribly unhappy about it to this day. As the capital city of a new Japan that espoused the values of Western civilisation, Tokyo continued to thrive. Commerce followed politics, and office buildings and suburbs started to spread beyond former boundaries.

Tokyo suffered terrible setbacks in the 20th century. The huge earthquake of 1923 caused almost 150,000 deaths and a massive amount of destruction. In 1944 and 1945, American bombing resulted in about 100,000 civilian casualties, with at least 1 million people displaced. Nevertheless, today, the Tokyo Metropolis area boasts a population of over 13.5 million, and is still growing while Japan's national population level is decreasing.

One of the most iconic modern buildings is Tokyo Tower, an orange-coloured Eiffel Tower-lookalike built in 1958. The 332.9m structure was built from the scrap steel of US tanks left behind after the Korean War. I love to point this out to American visitors, telling them, 'That's what peace can achieve'.

Many Britons say that London is not Britain. Americans may say that New York is not America. However, Tokyo will always be Japan and it will always lead, wherever Japan is heading.

Hokkaido 北海道

Hokkaido is the northernmost island of the Japanese archipelago, and is the home of the indigenous Ainu people (アイヌ), who settled there long before records began. The Ainu people resisted the cultural, political and racial amalgamation with the Japanese newcomers to the region – and their authority. In one such event, between 1669 and 1672, the Ainu rebelled against Japanese rule in an uprising known as Shakushain's Revolt (シャクシャインの戦い), named after the Ainu chieftain who led it.

Hokkaido further came to attention due to Imperial Russia's eastern expansion. The Tokugawa shogunate ordered a survey of Hokkaido in the late 18th century – except for the southern tip under the rule of the Kakizaki clan, the geographical details of the island were unknown. The map of Hokkaido was completed by Inō Tadataka (伊能忠敬1745–1818) in 1816, in a project that lasted some 16 years. The surveying expedition was met by their Russian counterparts at various points, marking the beginning of boundary disputes in these areas which continue today.

In the mid-19th century, the new government under the Meiji Restoration, continuing the policy of the Tokugawa shogunate, encouraged settlement in Hokkaido by subsidising pioneer farmers. As a result, peat marshes and barren landscapes were turned into farmland. To this day it is known as a foodie hotspot, with the likes of the Sapporo brewery gaining much attention for their beer.

Due to a historical lack of government interference and its relatively recent agricultural development, Hokkaido has an outlook unlike the rest of Japan. Its vast open spaces and wide skies are very different from typical Japanese countryside scenery, and there is a true frontier air about it.

Kyūshū 九州

Kyūshū is one of the four major islands of the Japanese archipelago, and consists of seven prefectures: Fukuoka (福岡), Saga (佐賀), Nagasaki (長崎), Kumamoto (熊本), Ōita (大分), Miyazaki (宮崎) and Kagoshima (鹿児島).

The north of Kyūshū, principally Fukuoka and Nagasaki, has been Japan's gateway to the outside world, and is the closest point to continental Asia. Since the 7th century, the central government in Kyoto maintained the city of Dazaifu (太宰府) in present-day Fukuoka to deal with foreign affairs, and it hosted embassies for Korea and China.

Nagasaki, with its complex coastline not unlike Norway's *fjords*, provided ports for vessels and a haven for pirates who raided Chinese coastal areas between the 13th and 16th centuries. The Portuguese arrived in the mid-16th century, and Nagasaki became the hub for trade. After the Portuguese were banned from Japan for their Christian missionary work, the Dutch monopolised Japanese–European trade from the nearby artificial island of Dejima (出島) – the only point of contact with the outside world in the closed country era – until Japan opened up again in the mid-19th century. Early 20th-century Nagasaki is also the setting for Puccini's opera *Madama Butterfly*.

In contrast, the rest of Kyūshū is generally rural, except for a number of factory towns. From its central region to the southern tip of Sakurajima (桜島) in Kagoshima, there are active volcanoes which provide the area with outstanding natural sights and *onsen* hot-spring resorts. The best known of Kyūshū's volcanoes are Mt Aso (阿蘇山) and Mt Sakurajima – both are still very active.

The city of Kagoshima, previously known as Satsuma (薩摩) – after which the citrus fruit was named – was one of the hotbeds for the revolutionaries who brought about the Meiji Restoration, and the volcanic activity of Sakurajima has forever been associated with the hot tempers of Kagoshima's citizens.

Okinawa 沖縄

Okinawa is the largest island in a chain of islands that create a 'dotted line' between the Japanese archipelago and Taiwan. The prefecture, also called Okinawa, is vast – the distance between its northernmost and southernmost points is about 400km, and from the easternmost to the westernmost, about 1,000km. That area is, of course, mostly ocean, and 90 percent of its approximately 1.5m population live on the main island.

The climate is tropical, the beaches beautiful, and the coral reefs endlessly inviting. In short, except for some nasty typhoons that make regular visits along the island chain, it is a paradise. However, history has been unkind to this idyll.

In the 15th century, the various clans of the islands were unified under a king, Shō Hashi (尚巴志 c.1371–1439). The kingdom of Ryukyu, as it was known, flourished as an intermediary trade port between Japan and China. To maintain the trading relationship, Okinawa remained a loosely tied tributary state of the reigning Chinese Ming dynasty.

At the beginning of Tokugawa shogunate, the warlord of Satsuma invaded Okinawa as a show of force. The conflict was brief and one-sided. The end result was that Okinawa became a dual tributary state to Japan as well as China, with Satsuma controlling the intermediary trade passing through Okinawa. China under the Qing dynasty (1636–1911) was somewhat indifferent to overseas matters, and as Satsuma's economic grip on Okinawa was harsh and strong, it shifted closer to Japan. Eventually, the full annexation of Okinawa ended its independent past, but brought modernisation to the islands.

During the Second World War, Okinawa was one of the fiercest battlefields in the Pacific theatre. Operation Iceberg commenced on 1st April 1945, with about 550,000 American and British soldiers making an amphibious attack on Okinawa Island, which was defended by about 116,000 Japanese soldiers. It ended three months later with about 180,000 Japanese deaths, half of which were civilian.

The Okinawan islands were put under American rule after the war, and remained so for nearly 30 years until 1972, when the area returned to Japan. However, the Americans remained, and Okinawa became the US base for the later Korean (1950–1953) and Vietnam (1955–1975) wars. With about 15 percent of Okinawa Island still occupied by US military today, and about 26,000 service members stationed there, Okinawans understandably wish to ease tensions in the region.

Chūgoku 中国

The Chūgoku region lies to the west of Kansai. It looks a bit like a tailbone attached to the biggest island of the Japanese archipelago, Honshū (本州). It consists of five different prefectures – Tottori (鳥取), Shimane (島根), Okayama (岡山), Hiroshima (広島), and Yamaguchi (山口).

The region is divided across the middle by a mountain range that stretches from east to west. As a result, the south and the north of this area have very different outlooks. The southern prefectures of Okayama and Hiroshima face the inland sea of Setonaikai. The northern prefectures of Tottori and Shimane face the comparatively rougher Sea of Japan. Yamaguchi prefecture, and the city of Shimonoseki (下関) at the westernmost tip, flourished as a toll collector for ships passing from the outer waters into Setonaikai and vice versa.

Yamaguchi was known as Chōshū (長州) in the Edo era, and together with Satsuma, was the main feudal fiefdom that brought down the Tokugawa shogunate. As such, it has a long political tradition going back to the Meiji Restoration.

The city of Hiroshima is the biggest in the region. Sadly, it is known internationally for being one of the two cities destroyed by atomic bombs during the Second World War (together with the city of Nagasaki). The main reason for Hiroshima being targeted was that it served the major naval port of Kure (呉) nearby. Hiroshima has thrived on shipbuilding and shipping industries, and is also the home to the carmaker Mazda.

Okayama is probably the most benign region of Japan. Historically, it has had the least number of typhoons and earthquakes than anywhere else in Japan. Okayama is also home to the picturesque city of Kurashiki (倉敷), with its rows of old Japanese-style warehouses – another testament to the region's shipping legacy.

Tottori and Shimane are somewhat isolated prefectures. In ancient times, however, they were important as they are close to the continental mainland. Izumo (出雲), in Shimane, is where the Izumo-taisha shrine (出雲大社) is located (its official name is *Izumo Ōyashiro*). It is dedicated to Ōkuninushi (大国主大神).

Shimane was also known for its Iwami Ginzan (石見銀山) silver mine. In the 16th and 17th centuries, Japan is said to have produced one third of the world's silver, and most of it came from this mine alone.

Tottori is the least populous prefecture of Japan and is known for its large sand dunes, Tottori *sakyu* (鳥取砂丘), which stretch for 16km of coastline.

Tōhoku 東北

The Tōhoku region spreads to the north of the Kantō region and is divided into six prefectures: Aomori (青森), Iwate (岩手), Akita (秋田), Miyagi (宮城), Yamagata (山形) and Fukushima (福島). Tōhoku literally means 'northeastern'.

Ever since the establishment of central government in Kyoto in the 7th century, the sovereignty of the Tōhoku region was an ambiguous affair. The strength of its independence was supported by several factors. Firstly, Tōhoku people at that time retained stronger ties with indigenous people. Secondly, they had gold. You can still witness this legacy in the Konjiki-dō of Chūson-ji (中尊寺金色堂) – a golden hall in the well-known Buddhist temple, which is covered with gold leaf inside and out.

Tōhoku's independence was surrendered completely when the samurai of Kantō, united under their leader, Minamoto no Yoritomo (源頼朝1147–1199), invaded Tōhoku in 1189 to bring the region under their rule.

Today, Tōhoku is perhaps Japan's best-kept secret in terms of tourism. With breathtaking natural scenery, excellent sake breweries and fascinating ancient places of worship such as Dewa Sanzan (出羽三山 – the Three Mountains of Dewa), which have long flourished as pilgrimage destinations. Local festivals, such as the Aomori *Nebuta Matsuri* (青森ねぶた祭), Miyagi's Sendai *Tanabata Matsuri* (仙台七夕まつり), and the Akita Kantō *Matsuri* (秋田竿灯まつり), are spectacular. You can also see samurai on horseback in full gallop at Fukushima's Soma-Nomaoi (相馬野馬追).

The love and pride that the people of Tōhoku hold for their region is so passionate and sincere that it is almost contagious – which makes Fukushima's nuclear disaster in 2011 all the more tragic. While the situation is fortunately contained, it will take a long time to heal. The diligence and resilience of those who work on the long mission of containment is yet another testament to the spirit of the people.

Tōkai 東海地方

The Tōkai region consists of the prefectures of Aichi (愛知), Gifu (岐阜), Mie (三重) and Shizuoka (静岡). Apart from landlocked Gifu, all face the Pacific Ocean.

Tōkai (東海) means 'eastern sea', and comes from the name for the ancient Tōkaidō coastal route (東海道 – 'eastern sea route') that stretched out of Kyoto towards Edo.

There is a ferry crossing from Ise (伊勢) in Mie to the area near what is now Nagoya (名古屋), the biggest city in the region. Ise is known for the Ise-Jingū (伊勢神宮), the mother of all Shinto shrines, dedicated to the sun goddess Amaterasu, and worshipped since time immemorial.

Nagoya, on the other hand, is of recent vintage. At the mouth of three rivers running from the mountains of the Japanese Alps, it is built on swampland made habitable after extensive flood control works in the 17th century. It is unofficially known as 'Toyota town', as the car manufacturing giant has its headquarters nearby.

Shizuoka is geographically wide. It stretches for 155km between its easternmost and westernmost points. At first glance, Shizuoka looks very rural. It is actually home to some world-famous motorbike manufacturers such as Honda, Yamaha and Suzuki. Yamaha began as a manufacturer of musical instruments and continues to sell them today, and its rival piano-maker Kawai is also based in Shizuoka.

Tōkai is blessed with a sunny climate, and as a result, it is famous for tea, oranges and eels. Nagoya is famous for *hitsumabushi*, its grilled eel on rice. Personally, I do not think much of it. As a Tokyo native, I naturally feel our way is the best.

Shikoku 四国

Shikoku is the smallest of the four major islands of the Japanese archipelago. It fits in like a jigsaw piece at the spot cornered by the western tail of Honshū and Kyūshū islands, with its southern edge facing the Pacific Ocean. Shikoku literally means 'four regions'. True to its name, it consists of the four prefectures of Tokushima (徳島県), Kagawa (香川県), Ehime (愛媛県) and Kōchi (高知県).

Kagawa is a lovely, sunny place and the birthplace of Kūkai (空海 774–835), the well-known leader of early Buddhism in Japan. The place is renowned for its *udon* noodles (うどん), which are made from wheat flour. *Sanuki* (讃岐), the old name for Kagawa, is synonymous with the noodle throughout Japan.

Tokushima lies at the eastern tip of Shikoku island and faces the strait that connects the Pacific Ocean to the internal sea of Setonaikai. The ebb and flow of the current between these bodies of water creates a famous whirlpool off the coast of Tokushima, known as *Naruto no Uzushio* (鳴門の渦潮).

Ehime is located in the north-western corner of the island. The place is warm and sunny, and known for producing various citrus fruits, especially *mikan* (みかん), more popularly known in the English-speaking world as tangerines.

Kōchi stretches along the whole southern coast of Shikoku island and faces the Pacific Ocean. It is best known for Sakamoto Ryōma (坂本龍馬 1836–1867), the famous revolutionary of the period leading up to the Meiji Restoration, who organised Japan's first modern, private merchant-navy company. His life was immortalised in a hugely popular novel, *Ryōma ga Yuku* (竜馬がゆく *Ryōma Goes His Way*) by Ryōtarō Shiba (司馬遼太郎 1923–1996), first serialised in the *Sankei Shimbun* (産経新聞) newspaper in 1962. Shiba's portrayal of Sakamoto became so popular and influential that there are still pilgrims who visit Sakamoto's enormous statue by the beach in Kōchi.

Kii Peninsula and other 'Power Spots'

A recent trend in Japanese domestic tourism is visiting what are called 'Power Spots' – locations that people believe to be auspicious for historical significance or natural beauty. The visitors are, presumably, blessed with good karma by seeing these places.

Perhaps one of the most popular destinations for Power Spot tourism is the Kii Peninsula (紀伊半島), on the island of Honshū. It spreads to the south of Osaka and Nara, and sticks out into the Pacific Ocean like a pregnant woman's belly. It is believed to have been created by huge ancient volcanoes, and it sits on a fault line.

Kii is close to political centres such as Nara and Kyoto, but is so dense with rainforest wilderness and mountain ranges that it was a natural destination for fugitives. Emperor Jimmu (神武天皇), the legendary first emperor of Japan, is said to have been repelled by those who occupied Nara so he sailed around the Kii peninsula and re-landed where the present-day town of Kumano stands and marched back onto Nara to claim victory.

The ancient roads from Kumano have become pilgrimage routes and are recognised as a UNESCO World Heritage Site.

Mt Fuji is another obvious 'Power Spot' destination, although it is inadvisable to attempt an ascent without proper planning and training. Yakushima Island (屋久島) in the southern tip of Kyūshū, with its wild rainforest and veteran cedar trees, is also very popular. The ancient capital of Nara also attracts many 'Power Spot' enthusiasts, as they believe, rather tenuously, that having been a capital city, there must have been some mysterious powers there. There are also several not-so-high mountains in Nara which are believed to be divine.

For those who cannot travel far from Tokyo, there is a famous 'Power Spot' in the middle of the city's business district. Masakado no Kubizuka (将門の首塚) is believed to be the spot where the severed head of a 10th-century samurai rebel is said to be buried. Taira no Masakado (平将門 died 940) was a local chief who conquered the whole of the Kantō region and declared himself a new emperor. He was killed in battle and his head was cut from his body to be displayed in Kyoto. Legend has it that the head flew across the sky like a rocket and landed on the spot upon which Masakado-zuka, literally meaning 'Masakado's mound', stands today.

Kōshin'etsu 甲信越

Kōshin'etsu (甲信越) is a subregion based on the old names of three prefectures: Kai (甲斐, now Yamanashi), Shinano (信濃, now Nagano) and Echigo (越後, now Nīgata). The name 'Kōshin'etsu' takes the first Chinese character of each, 'Kō (甲)', 'Shin (信)' and 'Etsu (越)'.

They are geographically large prefectures, but are mostly mountainous, and habitable land is very limited. Yamanashi basically consists of a basin surrounded by mountain ranges to the north, east and west, with its south side sealed by the colossal Mt Fuji. Due to this geography, massive snowfall in 2014 resulted in Yamanshi being cut off from the outside world. In a true demonstration of Japanese spirit, most major supermarket and convenience store chains competed to keep their shops open, mobilising helicopters to airlift merchandise despite the logistical difficulties. Yamanashi's soil is not naturally fertile and, as a result, its agriculture has traditionally excelled at value-added products such as fruit and, more recently, wine.

Nagano is sandwiched between the Hida and Akaishi mountain ranges. Its major cities and towns are dotted along the River Shinano, which runs through it. There is a long distance from north to south and this, along with the hilly landscape, prevent the mixing of people from each area within Nagano. Nagano was the host of the 1998 Winter Olympics, and is rightly famous for its ski resorts, combined with excellent hot spas. Like Yamanashi, Nagano is also into value-added agricultural products, with apples that are rightly prized for their juiciness. Chestnut sweets from the village of Obuse (小布施) are also a big deal.

Nīgata arches to the north, facing the Sea of Japan. Unlike Yamanashi or Nagano, Nīgata is a fertile place, with several rivers running through the land to the sea. With the ease of irrigation, Nīgata has become one of the top prefectures for rice production. Rice grown in the Uonuma (魚沼) area of Nīgata has consistently won prizes, and is known throughout Japan. With good rice and quality water, Nīgata is also teeming with sake brewers – cold winter months favour the brewing process. The area includes Sado Island (佐渡ヶ島), which floats in the Sea of Japan just off the coast. Gold was discovered in Sado at the beginning of 17th century, and its prolific production (at its peak, it produced around 400kg of gold per year) contributed to its economic stability throughout the Edo era. Production ceased in 1989.

What Makes
the Japanese

In the beginning...

Japan was first organised as a loose confederation of clans under the figurehead of an emperor or empress, and was finally brought together by a coup in 645, led by a prince, Naka-no-Ōe no-Ōji (中大兄皇子). The centralised national government realised it needed to bring together the numerous clan chiefs spread across the archipelago, who were mainly based in enclaves divided by the seas and mountain ranges, and who governed through complicated networks of alliances. A belief system in the form of shared stories, myths and legends was needed: a history.

The new imperial government recognised this spiritual side to their nation-building efforts. It was also thought that such an official history would bring legitimacy to the regime. The imperial family published two historical books: *Kojiki* (古事記 – *Records of Ancient Matters*) and *Nihon Shoki* (日本書紀 – *The Chronicles of Japan*). Both are probably the oldest books in existence in Japan. They are essentially anthologies of ancient stories which had come down the generations orally, maintained by professional storytellers who memorised the tales. Of course, the editors of *Kojiki* and *Nihon Shoki* did more than just write down the old stories. They *edited* the collections, from the creation myths to the immediate past, so they aligned with the ideals of the imperial lineage and its legitimacy to rule over Japan.

The official 'history' says that the Imperial Family are the descendants of the sun goddess Amaterasu (天照), one of the highest deities in Shintoism. They and their followers, *amatsu-kami* (天津神), or the 'heavenly gods', arrived from the celestial place to the land that is Japan, but did not find the place empty. It was occupied by the *kunitsu-kami* (国津神), gods living on earth, whose leader is known, among many other names, as Ōkuninushi (大国主).

The initial expeditions seem to have gone awry, with the invaders being seduced by aboriginal sirens and going native. After several attempts and some conflict, one of which tells the tale of the first sumo match between two braves each representing his side, Ōkuninushi finally concedes sovereignty to the goddess Amaterasu and her *amatsu-kami* on the condition that they build him the biggest shrine in the land. *Izumo-taisha* still stands today in Shimane (see page 23). Ōkuninushi's concession of sovereignty is depicted as a peaceful negotiation with minimum violence.

Spirituality

The introduction of Buddhism to Japan was very much a 'top-down' affair. It was an imported religion of immigrant technocrats, officially adopted by the emperor, who was aided and abetted by powerful factions in the governing elites.

The first wave of Buddhism reached its zenith in 752 with the building of a giant Buddha statue at Tōdai-ji (東大寺), in the then capital city of Nara (奈良). It is made of bronze, measures around 16m in height, and weighs in at a whopping 250 tons. Emperor Shōmu (聖武天皇 701–756) was a fervent believer, and ordered the construction of the giant Buddha as an act of appeasement in the hope of alleviating a smallpox epidemic and halting the natural disasters which blighted Japan during his reign. He also ordered the construction of a Buddhist temple in each of the provinces throughout his realm. However, this had more to do with efficient taxation for a massive construction project in the capital city than evangelism. Buddhism had more to do with filling the government coffers than saving souls at that time.

To fill the spiritual void, the Japanese had to wait for Kūkai (空海 774–835). The son of a minor nobleman of the aristocratic Saeki family, in Buddhism he sought spiritual fulfilment, rather than just knowledge. Kūkai managed to squeeze himself into the government's diplomatic mission to Tang China in 804 as an official student. There, he studied Vajrayāna, also known as Tantric Buddhism, which was the latest trend in Buddhist teaching. He was instructed by Huiguo (惠果 746–805), a Chinese monk who was the foremost authority on the subject.

Kūkai returned to Japan in 806, and the country soon went crazy for the Good News of Tantric Buddhism. It required faith to study and believe in the Buddhist Tantras, and to recite exotic-sounding utterances (mantras) in Sanskrit as the way to attain Nirvana. Faith had been missing from Japanese Buddhism until this point.

As Buddhism broke class barriers, a strange phenomenon started to happen in Japan's spiritual landscape: the people started to merge Shinto gods into Buddhism's theological context. The Shinto gods became, if not 'The Enlightened One', then at least sidekicks of The Enlightened One. Temples and shrines merged, and deities coexisted alongside each other in a weirdly comfortable way within Japanese spirituality. As the emperors were deemed the descendants of the sun goddess, the promiscuous mixing of Shinto gods with Indian deities became a bit of a theological embarrassment at a time when the role of emperor as the head of state came under the spotlight.

Zen Buddhism was another import from China, and centred on the teaching of meditation as the way to attain Nirvana. It became the religion for the new Samurai elites during the 12th century, at a time when the popularisation of Buddhism was steadily advancing. The life of ordinary people improved during the Kamakura period (12th–14th century), with advancement in agricultural methods and increased commerce aided by the adoption of currency. The ordinary people, unlike the stoic samurai, sought a little more from their religion than sitting down and as a result, forms of Buddhism gained popularity.

In the Age of Warring States (c.1467–c.1603), certain temples and religious groups gained considerable political and military power. Into this crucible of religious beliefs, the Jesuits made landfall with Christianity in the 1540s. The subversive doctrine of equality was always powerful and had been a common theme in all the religious beliefs which had come before, but this time it was stronger. The Jesuits' message of salvation was front and centre. When the persecution of Christians happened in the late 16th and early 17th centuries, they did not lack for martyrs.

When Tokugawa Ieyasu (徳川家康 1543–1616) became the first shōgun of Tokugawa in 1603, he was keenly aware of the need to contain religious zealots if peace was to be maintained. He ordered that everybody register with a temple of their choice by way of registering their citizenship – in effect, delegating civil administration powers to religious establishments. As an arm of governmental authority, the temples gained a steady source of income and lost their zeal for converting people.

This irreligiosity continues to this day. Visitors to Japan today are often confused by the apparent lack of consistency in our religious practices. We claim to be Buddhists, but marry in Christian churches, celebrate Christmas, and welcome in the New Year at Shinto shrines. If I could hazard a guess, our apparent nonchalance is only skin-deep, disguised by our tendency to subscribe to an 'every little helps' attitude when it comes to seeking supernatural intervention, and a preference of practical solutions over dogmatic inconveniences in the matter of faith. This can be seen from our merging of Buddhism and Shinto in the early days.

Geography and people

Japanese people believe in climate change. If the sea levels hadn't risen to submerge the land and separate continental Asia from the archipelago that would become Japan, you would still be able to walk from Korea to Japan. Indeed, you could still walk from China to Korea. You don't need a PhD in international relations to see the significance: geography creates history. But does geography define people?

Japan lies at the north-western corner of what is known as the Ring of Fire, the rim of the Pacific Ocean which experiences frequent earthquakes and volcanic eruptions as colliding tectonic plates slide deep into the underwater abyss. Japan is on top of the boundaries between *four* tectonic plates. It is the geoscientific equivalent of Tokyo's Shibuya Crossing but while Japan's active volcanoes and frequent earthquakes are challenging to say the least, these unique geological features have also blessed us with natural hot spas dotted across the country.

Weather-wise, Japan presents varying faces, from harsh winters in the northernmost Hokkaido, to the seemingly everlasting summer of Okinawa in the south. Nevertheless, we have one thing in common: sandwiched between the continental weather system over the Asian mainland, and the oceanic system over the Pacific, Japan's weather is constantly changing.

We have come to expect sudden and often violent climatic changes happening with very little foreshadowing. A.O. Scott, a film critic for the *New York Times*, once said that Godzilla, the Japanese fictional monster, is the epitome of our reverence for the natural force that is beyond human control or comprehension. Ultimately, nature cannot be tamed. In our fear and reverence for it, we have become fatalistic.

On the other hand, we have also learnt to enjoy the lulls between natural catastrophes. A life spent in fear is not a life well lived. In this sense, we have become pleasure-seeking and sensuous.

Women

'In the beginning, woman was the sun.'

Raichō HIRATSUKA (平塚 らいちょう 1886–1971), Japan's pioneering feminist.

One of the more striking features of Japanese society in what is called the early classical period between the 6th and 8th centuries is the ease with which a female ruler was accepted. In fact, during the 7th and 8th centuries, immediately prior to and following the coup of 645, Japan saw six empresses on the throne, reigning for more than 80 years in total.

Even in the early historical era, Japan was known to have female rulers. The earliest record of this comes from the official chronicle of the Chinese Wei Dynasty from between 220–265 (written sometime between 280 and 297). In it, Japan is described as a loose confederation of nations headed by the largest of them, Yamatai (or Yamato), and ruled by a shamanistic queen called Himiko.

It was probably believed and accepted by the ancient Japanese that female rulers had closer links with the gods than the male ones, even if their reigns entailed increased likelihood of succession problems.

The authors of the first official history of Japan had little difficulty recognising that the supreme deity in the native pantheon was female, because of the ancient memories of female spiritual leaders, as well as the presence of more recent female rulers. Under the circumstances, it was natural for them to declare that the imperial family had descended from the sun goddess, Amaterasu.

After nearly 700 years of government by the samurai, during which the emperors and empresses had been restricted to a merely symbolic role, a martial figure emerged in 1867: Emperor Meiji. This was intentional. To compete with Western imperialism, photographs of the emperor sporting a moustache and wearing a braided military tunic were thrust upon the Japanese people. We are still living in the shadow of this hyper-masculine image, which is a relatively modern fabrication.

Given the historical background, it is more than ironic that lawmakers are *still* arguing about whether or not to allow women to accede to today's Chrysanthemum throne.

The Emperor

The Emperor and his household are an enigma. The legend, first introduced in the 7th century is that the imperial linage goes all the way back to Emperor Jimmu, whose reign is supposed to have started in 660 BC. This is almost certainly a myth. That said, the lineage *does* go back to time immemorial, where written records are scarce. The official historical record from China's Three Kingdoms era (220–280 AD) notes that there was a series of kings and queens ruling the islands to the east – Japan.

At the time of the Meiji Restoration, it was a bit of a hard sell to reinstate the authority of an emperor. Ever since being sidelined by the government of samurai in the 12th century, emperors have been regarded as a relic of an ancient era. After 250 years of the Tokugawa shogunate's rigid grip on power, uniting the country under imperial authority was an idea cherished only by a number of revolutionaries. But it worked. Much effort was spent to revitalise the idea of an emperor as head of state.

Following defeat in the Second World War in 1945, the role of the Emperor came under scrutiny. As the head of state, Emperor Hirohito's responsibility for the war was impossible to deny. Still, the American conquerors were surprised to discover how little power Emperor Hirohito yielded in reality. Given the potential havoc to be expected as a result of the abolition of the emperor, and the fact that he played a big role in pacifying and uniting the war-torn Japanese immediately after the war, the position of emperor remained. His ancient mission to 'respect harmony' saved the tradition. Hirohito died in 1989, and is now referred to as Emperor Shōwa, named after the period in which he reigned.

For official courtly engagements such as annual rituals, weddings, and so on, members of the Imperial Family dress in costume from the Heian period (平安時代 794–1185), when the power of the household was paramount. They host the annual *Utakai Hajime* (歌会始), a traditional poetry reading event in early January. Anyone can enter the event in the hope of being presented to the Emperor and have his or her own poem read out loud. Japanese people enjoy such benign gestures that connect us to our unique history, tradition and culture.

Samurai

The Battle of Baekgang in 663 AD was a disaster for Japan. The Emperor had tried to revive the dynasty of Baekje on the Korean Peninsula against the allied forces of the (what would now be Korean) Silla dynasty and Tang dynasty of China. Japan lost badly, and following the defeat, the Emperor refrained from foreign wars. Once the threat of retaliation had waned, and public finances became a pressing issue, Japan decided to abandon the standing army. The loss of the military meant the absence of any policing force. Left to their own devices, farmers everywhere in Japan had to arm themselves for self-defence against outlaws. This was the beginning of the samurai.

While early samurai were to be found throughout Japan, the Kantō region, a flat (and at that stage, wet and marshy) area around present-day Tokyo, became the legendary birthplace of super-warriors known as *bando musha* (坂東武者), or 'Warriors of the East'.

In those times, Kantō formed the eastern border of the government in Kyoto. Beyond the region, to the north, were the lands belonging to the indigenous peoples whose allegiances to the emperor's authority were, at best, shifty. Minor skirmishes between the farmers of Kantō and marauding northerners were frequent. In the absence of a standing army, the emperor's general was forced to travel to Kantō only with his own private retinue, and then hire local warriors as mercenaries. All these circumstances provided ample opportunities for training, and many of the warriors excelled in martial skills.

The samurai choice of weapon was horseback archery. True, the Japanese produced magnificent swords, and continue to do so, but in practical fighting, nothing at that time could better the rapid hit-and-run of arrow shots from the back of a horse. Today, you can witness the mastery of this art, now known as *yabusame* (流鏑馬), by modern-day practitioners at festivals across Japan.

Eventually, samurai developed their own ethics and code of honour for, and among, themselves. They valued masculine qualities such as physical bravery, strength, loyalty, camaraderie, and manly outdoor pursuits like hunting. On the other hand, they abhorred cowardice, treachery and anything deemed effeminate. As history unfolded and society developed, the social mores of samurai changed, and their system of values became more complex.

Wabi-sabi

The Age of Warring States had a significant impact. The constant state of warfare for nearly 150 years left an indelible mark on the Japanese psyche, which manifested itself in a cultural and philosophical metamorphosis.

To grasp the topsy-turvy nature of the era, it's important to know that at the end of the era, Japan's leader was Toyotomi Hideyoshi (豊臣秀吉 1537–1598). He had been born a peasant and risen to the top to unify the country. He ordered the invasion of mainland Asia, bringing war to Korea. Japan is said to have possessed the biggest firepower in the world by the end of the period.

Like Europe, where civilisation developed at breakneck speed through the constant warfare of the 16th–18th centuries, Japan went through an unprecedented transformation. To support the constant war effort, which became increasingly more expensive, warlords encouraged the development of local commerce. Commercial cities, such as Sakai (堺), near present-day Osaka, flourished. The powerful needed the rich. In turn and by necessity, the powerful became rich themselves. In the end, Japan had a handful of rich and powerful warlords and their lieutenant samurai who found themselves as the new leaders of unified Japan.

Unfortunately, they were an uncultured lot. Literacy was low among fighting men and they were generally quite uncouth. The long absence of central authority created a fissure in Japanese cultural tradition. The new leaders had to find new traditions. The art of the tea ceremony provided the focal point for newly minted political and economic leaders seeking common cultural experience. It started among wealthy merchants in places like Sakai. Sen no Rikyū (千利休 1522–1591), considered the founder of the tea ceremony tradition that we know today, was a merchant of Sakai who is said to have traded in gunpowder. The tea ceremony was quickly picked up by the warlords and became fashionable. Soon, they were competing for the ownership of artefacts necessary to enrich their tea ceremony experiences, such as pottery, paintings and other paraphernalia.

Characteristically, Hideyoshi went to an extreme. He famously created a tea ceremony room in his residence which was made of gold, in an ostentatious show of his power and wealth. His tea ceremony was filled with exquisite porcelain imported from China.

Rikyū was Hideyoshi's instructor in the art of the tea ceremony, but frowned on his master's nouveau-riche tastes. In a brave artistic protest, Rikyū proposed new aesthetics to be observed in his style of tea ceremony, which were the opposite of Hideyoshi's ostentatious extravagances.

Rikyū called his aesthetic philosophy *wabi* (侘び) and *sabi* (寂び). *Wabi* refers to modest circumstances. Rikyū encouraged his followers to seek quiet satisfaction in less than opulent surroundings, and to find beauty in the modest beauty that shines more in contrast to its seemingly shabby environment. *Sabi* refers to internal quiet and peace. Rikyū proposed that true appreciation of beauty is borne out of the person's quiet contentment, rather than avarice.

In turn, Rikyū's philosophy of *wabi-sabi* formed the new basis on which Japanese culture was to flourish all the way to the present day.

Rikyū's artistic stand against Hideyoshi earned him the overlord's wrath for what the latter deemed was impertinence. In the end, Hideyoshi ordered Rikyū either to seek his forgiveness, or to commit suicide by way of punishment. Rikyū remained true to his belief and chose to take his own life. As a result, he was immortalised forever.

Wabi-sabi remains the cornerstone of the Japanese aesthetic. We continue to seek private happiness and contentment in the modesty and quietness which are, with a little effort, available to all, not just the rich and powerful.

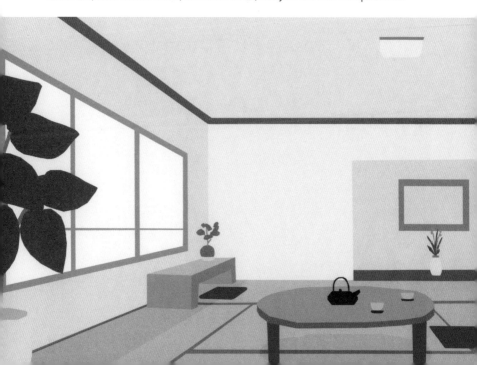

Ikigai
A JAPANESE CONCEPT MEANING A REASON FOR BEING

Satisfaction but feeling of uselessness

Delight and fullness, but no wealth

What you **LOVE**

PASSION

MISSION

What you are **GOOD AT**

Ikigai

What the world **NEEDS**

PROFESSION

VOCATION

Comfortable, but feeling of emptiness

What you can be **PAID FOR**

Excitement and complacency but sense of uncertainty

Ikigai

The Japanese are communal animals, not just social animals. People identify themselves very strongly in groups, whether that is in their workplaces, their families, alumni groups, teams they support, hobbies, and so on.

In Western stories, plots usually follow protagonists asserting their individuality against society – Billy Elliot finding his calling in dance despite the opposition of his family, or Rocky discovering the winner in himself despite the losers in his community. In Japan, typical stories go the other way. The Seven Samurai become a force through teamwork, while in *Spirited Away*, the main character starts the story as an indifferent girl, but develops into the lead role by insisting that she be allowed to work in the weird bathhouse of the fantasy world in which she finds herself.

This might have its roots in Japan's long agricultural tradition. It took a village to grow rice. Irrigation required village-wide compromise among community members as to the source and use of water. Planting and harvesting rice demanded village-wide cooperation. To be an outcast meant guaranteed starvation. The Japanese have a word for it: *murahachibu* (村八分). It literally means to divide a village into 80 percent. If someone is *murahachibu*, it means that the person has been ostracised by the majority of the community to which he or she used to belong.

Such allegiance to, and dependence on, a community used to be seen as one of the cultural traits that hindered the development of Japan into a more Western liberal society. It is true that the still-strong tradition of life-long employment has contributed to the rigid labour market in Japan, and continues to hinder the Japanese economy from realising its more dynamic potential. Nevertheless, there is no denying that acceptance into a community and recognition of one's contribution to it forms an important part of any individual's sense of his or her own worth. Even if that is only a part of a person's purpose in life, it gives that person a deep sense of satisfaction.

The Japanese call that satisfaction *ikigai* (生きがい): realising the value of one's life. The word is a combination of two separate words. *Iki* (生き) means 'life' or 'living', while *kai* (甲斐) means 'effect' or 'result'. A close translation in English would actually be a French phrase: *raison d'être*.

In a world of free agents living inside the comfort of their own bubbles, an increased sense of belonging and a search for *ikigai* may do more than a little good for the mindset of the global community.

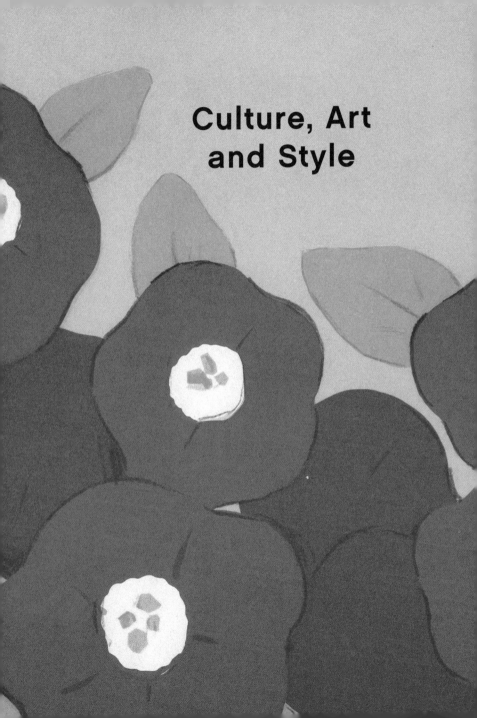

Culture, Art and Style

Words with no direct translation

Most Japanese words and expressions that can't easily be translated into English share some common traits: they are generally expressions which recognise and reinforce the communal ties that bind people, or they relate to a typically Japanese philosophy.

For example...

いただきます You say **itadakimasu** before you start a meal, just as you might say *bon appétit* in French, but it is a word of thanks for what you're about to eat. The literal translation is 'Allow me to have this for myself', which expresses modesty as well as gratitude. The gratitude directed not only towards the host and cook, but also the farmers, fishermen, and even natural phenomena such as sunshine and rainfall, that all contributed to the creation of the meal.

ごちそうさまでした At the end of a meal, say **gochisōsama-deshita**. The word *chisō* (馳走) originally referred to the task of acquiring all the ingredients necessary for a feast, so the literal translation is something akin to, 'What a *chisō* it must have been!'. In other words, 'Thank you so much for making the necessary effort to prepare such a splendid meal'. It is an expression of gratitude directed at the host and cook.

おつかれさま **Otsukaresama** is an acknowledgement of someone's hard work. The direct translation is 'You must be tired' – but the tiredness does not have a negative connotation. Rather, it is the natural state for someone who has laboured long and hard for the benefit of a task. You are giving that person recognition for their contribution.

おすそわけ **Osusowake** means 'sharing the hem' – but makes no sense in the context of western clothes. The hems of a kimono are always divided left and right, until you close the front and tie it at the waist with an *obi* belt. Some linguistic acrobatics are required here, but *osusowake* means that you share a gift with someone else, just as the hem of a kimono always flows away to the left and right. If you receive a box full of apples from a family member who is a farmer, you would share some of them with your neighbour, saying 'This is *osusowake*', giving it the nuance that this is not a special gift, but the mere sharing of our good fortune, as naturally as the hem of a kimono flows both ways.

おかげさま A translation of **okagesama** is 'Thanks to you', but the Japanese use this expression for almost everything. If someone recognises that you have recovered from a common cold, you could reply '*Okagesama*', or, 'Thanks to you, I have recovered' – even if that person hasn't had anything to do with your cold at all. What you are recognising is not a specific causation or contribution made by the addressee, but the connection that both of you have by belonging to the same community. It is similar to the English poet John Donne's principle of 'No man is an island'.

つまらないものですが Say **tsumaranai mono desuga** when you are giving a gift. Paradoxically, it means 'This is such an uninteresting thing'. The Japanese, not wishing to make a recipient feel obliged, downplay the value of a gift. It is the show of modesty that lubricates social interactions.

お邪魔します **Ojama shimasu** is similar in spirit to *tsumaranai mono desuga* and is used when you are invited to someone's home. Literally, it means 'I will be a disturbance to you'. Of course, this is not a declaration of one's intention to raise hell in somebody else's abode – it is simply a show of modesty by way of giving thanks for the invitation and to reassure the host that you will be careful not to cause unnecessary inconveniences.

おたがいさま The direct translation of **otagaisama** would be 'As you are, I am', or 'As you do, I do'. If someone apologises to you for being late, you say '*otagaisama*' to convey the sentiment of 'not to worry, it could have easily been me who was late'.

寂しいい **Sabishii** refers to a typical Japanese philosophy. *Sabi* is the same word used in *wabi-sabi*, and is an aesthetic philosophy that refers to a state of incompleteness. This may refer to the absence of a person, as in 'I miss you', or simply a general state of resignation as to the imperfect nature of the world around us.

仕方ないい The nearest translation of **Shikata-nai** is 'It cannot be helped'. *Shikata* means a way, method or means and *Nai* denotes the absence thereof, so together they translate as 'There is no way'. This may sound negative to an unaccustomed ear, but it is an expression of resigned acceptance of what has come to pass. This philosophy helps renewal and regrowth in a country where natural geography and climate can result in sudden violent earthquakes, typhoons and volcanic eruptions. In this way, the expression has a certain therapeutic value for people, when faced with uncertainty.

風情 **Fuzei** describes an aesthetic appeal that can be applied to scenery, artistry and people. This is different from mere 'beauty'. The closest English term would probably be 'style', but this Japanese word is often used to describe a state that is not obviously pleasing. A ragged coastline in stormy weather, the early morning mist rising silently in a forest, well-used tea cups, or even an old lady's wrinkled hands can all be described as *Fuzei-no-aru*, or 'full of Fuzei'. This is a compliment borne out of a very Japanese philosophy of value beyond sheer beauty.

粋 or 意気 **Iki** was traditionally a word associated with the common people of Edo (Tokyo) during the Edo Period, particularly in the 18th and 19th century. It is a word used to describe city residents or urban folk, who typically have a lively, although not necessarily extravagant, lifestyle. The term is also associated with tidiness and cleanliness.

Waka: poetry as a social skill

Somehow, ancient Japanese people decided their language sounded better – more rhythmical and meaningful – when uttered in groups of five and seven syllables. It was the birth of Japanese poetry, or *waka* (和歌).

The structure of these poems differed wildly in the early days. Some were longer, line after line of five- and seven-syllable combinations, but later the 5-7-5-7-7 structure emerged as standard.

In the courtly life of the Heian period (8th–12th century), writing *waka* became an important social skill, especially in relation to matters of the heart. Both men and women were judged for their character and intelligence on their ability to compose these poems. Court ladies led secluded lives deep in their residences, surrounded by their ladies-in-waiting. Suitors only caught glimpses of them, and assumed their physical beauty by reputation. To initiate courtship, a man had to send a well-crafted poem declaring his desire to be more intimately acquainted with the lady. The lady favoured the man with a reply also in the form of poetry. To indicate 'I am not that into you', the reply might have been written by one of her ladies-in-waiting, reminding the suitor of the inappropriateness of the match. If the initial poem was well written and the author was of good repute, the lady herself might have composed a reply and, better still, written it herself on suitably stylish stationery. It was important that these poems were witty and showed the author's intelligence and education. For this purpose, lesser men and women of letters had to collect noted poets among their staff or ladies-in-waiting to act as ghostwriters and literary advisers.

With his passion now whipped into a frenzy, the suitor would make a daring nocturnal visit to the lady. If the match was deemed appropriate, the gates would open and the lovers would spend a night of passion together.

It was regarded as bad form for the man to stay late into the morning – he was expected to beat a retreat in the morning mist. Still, the most important task remained. The man had to compose yet another suitably tender poem to his lady. It was called *kinuginu no uta* (後朝の歌), literally a 'morning-after poem'. It was basically a thank-you note to praise the lady's beauty and express the sorrow of parting. It was important for this to reach the lady promptly, as any tardiness suggested disappointment on the man's part. There is a tale of a man who neglected to send the morning-after poem, which resulted in his distraught lover becoming a nun. Had Shakespeare's Ophelia been Japanese, she would not have wasted her time picking flowers.

If the courtship went well and the lovers became a steady couple, they announced their partnership publicly with a ceremony called *tokoro arawashi* (床顕し), literally meaning 'exposing the bed'. They were then regarded as husband and wife by society. This was the form of marriage amongst Heian aristocrats. The wife would remain with her family, and any children resulting from the match were raised with her family as well.

There were 21 anthologies of *waka* poems assembled at the emperor's command between the 10th and 15th centuries, each representing the style, taste and fashion of poetry at the time.

秋山に落つる黄葉しましくは
な散り乱ひそ
妹があたり見む

On this autumn mountain
Tumbling yellowed leaves
For just a moment
Cease your scattering
For I would see my beloved's home.

Author unknown, c. AD 759

行く春や
鳥啼き魚の
目は泪

Spring is passing.
The birds cry, and the fishes fill
With tears in their eyes.

Bashō, 1689

Haiku

In the literary parlour game *renga* (連歌), or 'chain of songs', the 5-7-5-7-7 syllable structure of *waka* is divided into two. The first person composes the 5-7-5 part, and the second person completes the poem by adding their own 7-7. The next person then plays on this first collaborative piece by adding another 5-7-5, developing the theme proposed in the first set, and another person adds 7-7 lines. This goes on among the participants for a predetermined number of times, usually 100.

During the Heian period, people held *renga* parties where the host and guests brought their individual literary tastes and education into creating this collaborative art and contest of *bons mots*. *Renga* contributed greatly to the development of Japanese literary culture and it spread among the populace. It continued to be popular well into the Edo period, but in the 17th century another trend occurred in which only the first 5-7-5, or *hokku* (発句), began to stand on its own as a composition. This was the birth of *haiku* (俳句).

As poetry became popularised through its various forms and context, there was a tendency of the tone of composition to become less arty and more, for the lack of a better word, vulgar. For an English speaker, it would have been as if people had stopped aspiring to Shakespeare's sonnets and settled for concocting funny limericks instead. Witticism and clever punchlines were valued over artistic sensibilities.

The comedic *haiku*, called *senryū* (川柳), remains popular today, but was limiting the potential of new shorter forms of poetry. The poet who changed this slide was Matsuo Bashō (松尾芭蕉 1644–1694). He gained fame and fans through witty compositions, very much in keeping with the fashion of the time. Nevertheless, he dispensed with the popularity and pursued the *haiku* compositions which reflected his own artistic sensibilities and personal feelings. Luckily for him, his movement gathered strength during his lifetime.

Haiku continues to be popular in modern Japan. All major newspapers in Japan invite readers to submit their compositions on a regular basis, and professional *haiku* masters select and publish the ones they like.

The popularity is based on two things. One is simplicity – the 5-7-5 structure is accessible to all, and does not require arduous mental labour for composition. The second is the freedom of its subject matter – Bashō's movement allowed people's ordinary feelings to be expressed in poetic style. It can be funny and witty, or sombre and intelligent. It has become a true popular art.

Kabuki theatre

The social upheaval created by the Age of Warring States (between the 15th and 17th centuries) gave people room to express their individuality. When the era drew to a close and peace returned, commerce flourished and people were hungry for entertainment. Kyoto regained its status as Japan's capital, and entertainers gathered on the riverside of the nearby Kamo River, which was regarded as being outside the city's jurisdiction.

One of the more famous performers was a female dancer and impresario called Izumo no Okuni (出雲阿国 born c.1572), who gained fame by staging what she called *kabuki odori* or '*kabuki* dance'. The word *kabuki* (歌舞伎) is derived from the verb *kabuku*, meaning 'to lean' or 'to be out of the ordinary'. *Kabuki* in this context was used to denote a show's outrageousness – it is said that performances were very erotic in tone. Before long, female performers were banned by the authorities. However, the show went on, as they say.

From the start, the essence of *kabuki* has been its popular appeal. Actors don outrageous costumes and wear eye-catching make-up. The more extravagant the stage sets, the better the audience's appreciation.

Kabuki continues to be popular in Japan today, and many *kabuki* actors work in film and TV. However, one of the unfortunate features of *kabuki* theatre is its hereditary system. There are a number of *kabuki* actor families, and famous actors' names are usually passed on from father to son. Therefore, we have Ichikawa Ebizō XI, Nakamura Kanzaburō XVIII and Onoe Kikugorō VII, for example. Name succession is a big event in *kabuki* theatre, and fans debate endlessly whether or not a young star is ready to fill his predecessor's shoes. It maintains prestige and is a nice gimmick for promoters. Still, the sense of tradition can prevent fresh talents from shining, and is terribly anachronistic.

Having said that, a visit to a *kabuki* theatre is a treat. *Kabuki-za* (歌舞伎座), a theatre in the Ginza district of Tokyo, has been recently renovated to a fine standard. You don't have to stay for the whole performance, and can go in for just one act. I heartily recommend a visit to bask in the glory of this 'anything goes' show-business world.

Architecture: from shrines and temples to castles

Despite the land being prone to devastating natural disasters, Japan boasts many well-preserved historical buildings. In the Confucian-influenced Chinese tradition of *Tian Ming*, or the 'Mandate of Heaven', any representations of past power, especially buildings, were likely to be destroyed by a new emergent power by way of a celebratory bonfire for the refreshed 'mandate'. The Japanese have always been more frugal, maintaining and reusing old buildings, seeing spiritual significance in structures which have survived through the thick and thin of historical upheaval.

Thanks to this tendency to preserve old buildings, historic buildings in Japan look a lot more ancient than their Chinese or Korean equivalents, even though Japanese history is much younger. For a Japanese national style to emerge, the Chinese style had to be adapted to suit Japan's climate and lifestyle. This primarily meant building for the sit-on-the-floor style of living and so Japanese houses tended to be built with lower ceilings and roofs. Another common feature is a raised floor, which prevents humidity from seeping through from the earth to the building. This style is exemplified in Shōsō-in (正倉院), a treasure house in Nara prefecture.

Another original Japanese invention was the castle. During the Age of Warring States, warlords built castles to protect their territories. To maintain the defensive strength of such buildings, they adopted stonewalls, moats, tiled roofs, earthen walls, elaborate defensive plans and labyrinthine designs. To top it all off, warlords started building towers, or donjons, called *tenshukaku* (天守閣), as the centrepiece of castles. The structure, with its elaborate design combining roofs, eaves and gables to make it look even taller, demonstrated and symbolised the power and authority of the warlords and became an essential part of the Japanese architectural scenery. One example is the well-preserved Himejijō (姫路城), a castle in Hyōgo prefecture.

Contrary to the tender love and care the Japanese have given to their ancient buildings, Japan's modern constructions are scrap-and-build affairs. With the extreme urbanisation that has occurred in the last century or so, and the easing of building height restrictions, cities are growing upwards, as well as becoming more energy efficient. It will, I think, take several decades more for the definitive modern Japanese style of architecture to emerge.

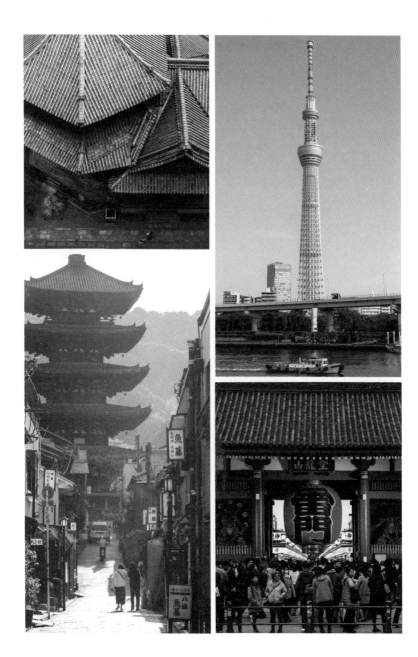

Celebrity culture

In Japan, regular television broadcasts started in 1953, and TV sets became very popular in Japanese households around the time of the Tokyo Olympics in 1964.

Prior to the dominance of TV, celebrities came from the film industry. However, while actors commanded the adoration of fans, their exposure was limited. With the advent of TV, they were able to appear on peoples' screens each week, or in some cases, every day. The demand for TV personalities – actors, comedians or mere presenters – became huge.

The demand was met by agencies who managed such personalities, called *talento* in Japanese English. The number of such instant *talento* celebrities increased in direct inverse correlation to the actual talent possessed by those going before the cameras.

In the 80s, stressed-out TV executives happened upon a brilliant idea. They realised that those appearing on TV did not have to be special in any way. Amateur singers, slapstick comedians and other entertainment talents (to use all those words in the loosest possible way) flooded the airwaves. Japan was decades ahead of the reality show trend in the West.

More recently, with a plethora of TV celebrities scraping the bottom of the ever-decreasing money pot of the entertainment industry, the market was flooded with manufactured and autotuned music known as *J-pop*. If a single voice cannot hold an audience (let alone a tune), they are packaged together as various boy and girl groups in true cheaper-by-the-dozen fashion. One of the most extreme examples is, AKB48, a girl group which has more than 100 members (the 48 refers to the original number of members in 2005).

After decades of this business model, the quality of entertainment on Japanese TV is beyond low. Dramas are either reruns, remakes or copies of past hits. As ratings decline, so does advertisement revenue, resulting in even direr production quality. At the same time, those *talento* agencies are coming under scrutiny due to exploitative contracts and harsh business practices.

Still, TV stations are using their lobbying powers with politicians, who cannot stoop low enough to get positive televisual exposure, to stifle competition. As a result, Japan has not seen any new competitors entering the TV business since the 60s.

In any event, the current status quo cannot be maintained for long. It is a veritable clattering train with no one in charge.

Kimono

Kimonos were everyday wear well into the Meiji period (1868–1912) and Taishō period (1912–1926). Western-style clothes, such as suits for men and dresses for women, were reserved for office work and special occasions. However, these Western styles became increasingly popular, especially after the introduction of casual clothes following the Second World War, and the roles reversed. Gradually, kimonos came to be worn only for special occasions, such as New Year's Day celebrations, for Coming of Age Day in mid-January by people who have reached the age of 20, weddings, and so on. As a result, kimonos became ornate and very expensive, to be fit for the special occasions for which they were to be worn. The casual kimono nearly disappeared from the marketplace.

This trend reversed in the 1990s. It started with yukata (浴衣), casual kimonos for the summer season which became fashionable among young women. Yukatas are cheaper than a full kimono set, and are a nice way to stand out from the crowd. Following this initial spark, there was a boom for recycled kimonos in the 2000s.

The Western-style clothes market is saturated with brand names in an industry that promotes changing trends each season. Consumers end up paying too much for the clothes, only to look like everybody else in accordance with the fashion diktat of the day. Kimonos are a good way out of this uniformity.

Being out of fashion for some time, there are few rules about the way one is supposed to wear a kimono. One is allowed freedom of expression in choosing their style – there are even kimonos made of denim.

Personally, I like the kimono because I feel it is designed to make ordinary people look good. However, one drawback may be that kimonos do not do winter very well.

Harajuku girls

Tokyo developed from east to west. To the west of the city spread the pastoral lands owned mostly by temples and shrines, where tenant farmers grew vegetables for the ever-increasing city dwellers. As the city was developing, Harajuku (原宿) was an inn town (宿) in that countryside.

Following the Meiji Restoration of the mid-19th century, the area to the north of Harajuku (present-day Yoyogi Park [代々木公園]), became the training ground for the army. After the Second World War, the same area was appropriated by the Americans for their military barracks. For the first time in its history, this brought to the area some semblance of 'cutting edge', with the presence of 'exotic foreigners'.

In 1964, the Olympic Games were held in Tokyo, and the now formerly American area was turned into Yoyogi National Gymnasium, as well as the athletes' village. Harajuku had come under the spotlight as a smart area with an air of modernity and international sophistication, with the nearby 'park life' in Yoyogi Park, a concept which was alien to most Japanese at that stage. In the 1970s, with post-war economic growth flourishing into a blustering consumer culture, a commercial complex was built that housed many boutique fashion labels, designer shops – Harajuku was put firmly on track to become the fashion hub that it is today.

Shops, cafés and art spaces continued to pop up in the area. In the 1980s, the local council closed certain streets to traffic in the area and made them pedestrian-only at weekends. This attracted buskers and group dancers, with one well-known tribe known as *takenoko-zoku* (竹の子族), meaning 'Bamboo-shoot people' (don't ask me why). They dressed outrageously, but somehow danced in unison, in a true Japanese tribute to homogeneity. The area attracted more than 100,000 people a day at its height and these crowds led the authorities to cease the pedestrian-only days in 1998. The musicians, dancers and other event-goers moved to Yoyogi Park and its surrounding areas.

Harajuku continues to attract fashion-industry types, and it is the place to gauge trends, launch new concepts and test new brands. Its reputation as the cutting edge of Japanese fashion attracts tourists from all over the world, creating a global vibe. You can see edgily dressed young women going window shopping on any given day in Harajuku, although these days you cannot automatically assume they are all Japanese. That's just another snapshot of the place, which has gone through many reinventions of itself in its short history.

Ninja

The history of ninja goes back a long way. The word literally means 'spy', and the history of spying and the use of clandestine means to achieve victory in wars is as old as the history of warfare itself.

For spies to flourish, there has to be a state of war or at least the threat of it. The Age of Warring States in Japan provided an ideal background. Samurai warlords divided the country into their separate fiefdoms and vied for survival.

However, the culture and traditions of the samurai did not suit the clandestine work demanded of spies. Each samurai clan was guaranteed the safety of their person and property in return for their allegiance to the warlord. Battles were important opportunities for samurai to prove their allegiance and to gain reward for their valour. For this purpose, their actions in battle had to be conspicuous and recognised. Samurai of earlier times used to make a speech before going to fight, ensuring that not only enemies, but comrades knew of their presence and the deeds which were about to be committed. Even when mass infantry fighting became the norm, samurai warriors found a way to get noticed, decorating their armour extravagantly so everybody was aware of their presence. In short, samurai made poor ninja.

Because of this, warlords had to rely on people outside the samurai class for clandestine work. In the lulls between wars, the task usually fell to monks and performing artists who could cross the boundaries of the warlords' spheres of influence relatively easily.

In times of battle, warlords could not avail themselves of monks or performers conveniently travelling around the battlefields. To gather information and carry out clandestine missions, warlords had to rely on low-class samurai.

Constant warfare sustained the demand for such specialists, and two regions became known for supplying more skilled professionals than any other. One was Kōga (甲賀), in present-day Shiga Prefecture (滋賀県). The other was Iga (伊賀), in present-day Mie Prefecture (三重). They were both relatively close to Kyoto to get the latest news, and their lands were mountainous.

The appeal of the ninja is that they were little people with extraordinary skills, fighting against the harshness of life and the tide of time. In typical tales, they fight against the inevitable coming of the authoritarian Tokugawa shogunate. Through such stories, ninja realise everyday fantasies in fictional settings.

Pottery

As in any other civilisation, pottery can tell us a lot about a country's origins and history. However, for an East Asian country such as Japan, the history of pottery tells a story that is more nuanced and longer than many others. This is because China, as our local hegemon, placed inordinate value and importance on pottery, particularly the porcelain variety. Chinese pieces were so extraordinary that it is still synonymous with porcelain art today.

Japan, as ever, followed China's lead in such cultural matters, and learned to love the fine art of pottery beyond its mere utility. It was, however, an impossible task for provincial Japanese artisans to match the technology and sophistication of the objects coming from China's official imperial kilns. Consequently, fine porcelain pieces were imported to Japan and became highly valued possessions of the wealthy. Japanese artisans had to console themselves with being poor imitators of China's majestic creations.

The tradition of the tea ceremony and its champion, Sen no Rikyū changed perceptions of Japanese pottery forever. Rikyū proclaimed that beauty did not reside only in the flawlessness of imported Chinese porcelain, but also existed in the simple, earthly, unsophisticated pottery of Japanese artisans. His belief was a manifestation of his *wabi-sabi* philosophy of finding beauty and value in imperfection, simplicity and understatement.

Under the patronage of tea masters such as Rikyū, his followers and successors, Japanese pottery found its own aesthetic and confidence, which flourishes to this day. Credit is also due to China, for being such a huge global presence in pottery. To compete, the Japanese had to innovate not just their technology, but their aesthetic philosophy.

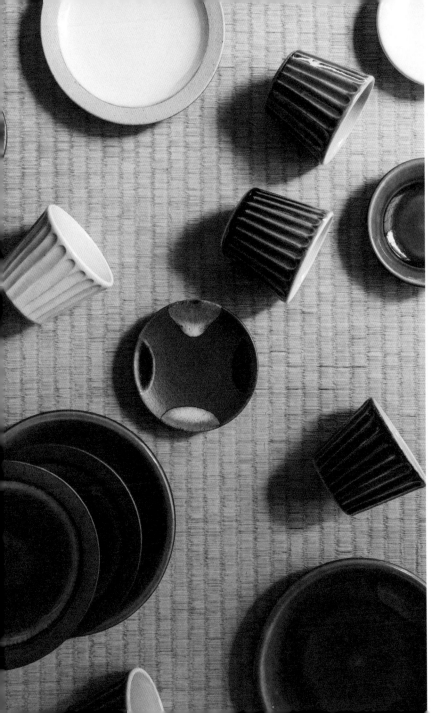

Kintsugi

Kintsugi is a traditional method of fixing broken pottery – but one that has become an artform in its own right.

Historically, pottery was vitally important to people. While it was used as an everyday essential household tool for storage and cooking, it took an enormous amount of labour and skill to create. Imported Chinese pottery was mainly a veritable treasure due to its artistry. So, naturally, people wanted to be able to mend their precious pots if they broke (this was long before the wastefulness of modern consumerism arrived).

Urushi (漆) – sap from the Chinese lacquer tree – was mainly used for lacquerware, to beautify as well as strengthen woodcrafts. It was also useful as an adhesive. With the advancement of lacquerware technology and aesthetics in the 15th and 16th centuries, fixing pottery with *urushi* also became artistic. Repairers started to decorate the trace of a fracture where *urushi* was applied with colouring agent such as gold or silver powder, making geometric patterns on the finished product. This method was named *kintsugi*, literally meaning 'putting together with gold'.

Appreciation of *kintsugi* was born out of the tradition of the tea ceremony. In particular, Sen no Rikyū, that tea master extraordinaire, praised *kintsugi* as the manifestation of his *wabi-sabi* philosophy. For Rikyū, *kintsugi* represented the honest presentation of simple artefacts. It told a story: the story of the pot, the loving care its owner had shown to it which necessitated its repair, and the skills and artistry of the repairer. For Rikyū, the imperfection of *kintsugi* pottery was to be cherished for its simple honesty.

Furuta Oribe (古田織部 1544–1615) was a minor warlord who became known as an ardent follower of Rikyū and his art of tea ceremony. Impressed by Rikyū's love of *kintsugi*, Oribe started to break his treasured collection of ceramics to make them into *kintsugi*. Informed of Oribe's devotional vandalism, Rikyū reprimanded him, telling him that the true value of *kintsugi* is not in its outward appearance or achieved intentionally through such violent acts. For Rikyū, Oribe's destruction and reconstruction represented contrived and twisted vanity, which was the opposite of what he valued in *kintsugi* and his 'let it be' philosophy.

At the Table

The impact of tea

Tea is arguably China's greatest gift to the world. It was first introduced to Japan around the 9th century at the height of the glorious Tang dynasty, one of those many periods when all of Asia looked to China as the fount of civilisation and culture. However, once the Tang dynasty went into decline, the first tea-drinking boom in Japanese history waned.

Tea's renaissance in Japan began towards the end of the 12th century, thanks to a monk called Eisai (栄西), who studied the latest Buddhist trends in China's Song dynasty. When he returned to Japan, he came with the seeds and sapling of a tea tree, and the latest trend in Buddhist teaching, Zen Buddhism.

The powerful merchant class of Sakai collectively ran an independent, autonomous city much like Venice. One member of that class was Sen no Rikyū who became the greatest of tea ceremony masters.

Rikyū's tea ceremony, in its essence, is the organising of a party. The host invites the guests to enjoy tea made by that host. However, all the processes must be carried out along the basis of aesthetics rooted in Zen Buddhism. The invitation, handwritten with a traditional Japanese brush, must be pleasing both to read and look at. The guests arrive at the appointed place to observe the garden fully prepared, but not artificially manicured like a flower garden. Zen Buddhism sees beauty in the harmony between nature and the host's intent to welcome and please the guests.

The meals provided to the guests before the tea is served are called *kaiseki-ryōri* (懐石料理), which literally means 'cuisine of stone held to the body'. The meal cannot be a gluttonous feast, because Zen Buddhism abhors excess. The guests are then guided to a teahouse, which can only be entered through a small entrance, forcing the guests to kneel, thereby removing any pretence of social hierarchy. The furniture is basic and bare, with one piece of art or nature, perhaps a flower, adorning the wall to symbolise the theme of the event or a connection with the world outside the small room in which all now sit. The water boils in a simple cast-iron kettle over a fireplace cut in the floor, and the tea is prepared in a ceramic bowl.

The art of this style of tea ceremony is practised by men and women, young and old, to this day. An art critic once called it the 'art of peace' which has been the source of spiritual nourishment for the Japanese people and their arts.

Dashi: the umami of everything

Truth be told, we Japanese should doff our caps to China for anything culinary. They have been at it for over 4,000 years. Constant effort has been poured into their pursuit of gastronomy, coupled with the search for a healthy diet. Chinese vocabularies are full of cooking-related words.

Compared to this cooking titan on our doorstep, Japan's food traditions are naturally modest. That said, nothing compares to home cooking, and we take pride in what we have to offer.

Chief among our proud traditions is the discovery of *umami* (旨味). *Umami* is usually translated into English as 'savoury taste', but it is so much more than that. It is the taste in foods that is neither sweet, sour, salty, nor bitter, but nevertheless forms an essential part of a full palate. It comes from the variety of amino acid combinations.

Japanese people use various ingredients to extract *umami*. Usually, we boil sea kelp seaweed (*kombu* 昆布), or dried bonito fish (*katsuobushi* 鰹節) to make a broth which we call *dashi* (出汁). *Dashi*, literally meaning 'extracted soup', is full of *umami* and is used as a base in a number of dishes.

We have been using *dashi* for centuries, but *umami* was only discovered and scientifically analysed at the beginning of the 20th century by chemistry professor Kikunae Ikeda (池田菊苗 1864–1936). He co-founded a company to produce the *umami* seasoning called Ajinomoto – the original producer of monosodium glutamate (MSG).

Compared to other tastes, such as saltiness and sweetness, *umami* is subtle. Perhaps for this reason, it is regarded as a sign of a sophisticated palate to appreciate it.

Sake: old drink, new industry

When Japan was first described in the Chinese official chronicle in the 3rd century, it noted that Japanese people liked to drink. They got that right. So, it appears that the Japanese knew how to make sake from rice quite early on and it was drunk by all in large quantities.

In the Heian period (8th–12th century), the court in Kyoto brewed its own sake. But the better ones were made by the priests in temples – nothing, it seems, makes for better alcohol than holy thoughts.

The nationwide sake-making boom had to wait until the Kamakura period (12th–14th century), when the advance in agricultural output made it possible for the farmers to set aside an extra yield of rice for sake making.

As sake production requires a steady rice supply, and a distribution and sales network, brewers became prototype capitalists. They were the wealthy local landowner types who could produce and/or buy up the necessary rice. The brewing work that took place during wintertime following the harvest also provided good opportunities for tenant farmers during the slack season, and some of them became specialist master sake makers, known as Toji (杜氏), hired for their expert skills by the highest bidder.

The end of the Second World War ushered in a dark period for sake when cheap, bad quality and sometimes downright dangerous alcohol made its rounds on the black market. The makers did their best to recover from this nadir, through fairs and competition between brands. Scientific advances also helped.

Although the economic environment surrounding sake makers is not getting any easier, it is safe to say that we are now drinking a better quality sake than at any other time in history. Nevertheless, apart from a group of major producers in Nada and Kyoto, sake makers still tend to have small, local businesses that are vulnerable to any whim of economic adversity.

Sake can be divided into categories of Junmai, Ginjo and Dai-Ginjo, depending on the amount of polishing the rice goes through at the beginning of the process. These categories are, in fact, of recent invention and are part of a sales effort by sake makers to differentiate their products. Although Ginjo and Dai-Ginjo were prized at first for their clearer tastes, achieved through extensive rice polishing, some prefer Junmai for its characterful palate.

In a way, for the resilience and innovation of all involved, sake is a typically Japanese product that we can responsibly be proud of, without the need for moderation.

Pesco-vegetarian Japan

Somehow, livestock farming didn't take off in Japan until modern times. The consumption of meat was limited to fish, chicken and occasional game. This is very odd considering that the Chinese table is not complete without pork or some other kind of meat, and that, historically speaking, the Japanese more often than not followed where the Chinese led.

The absence of meat from traditional Japanese food culture is most probably due to Buddhist influence. Although there was never a religious taboo about eating meat, Buddhist monks thought it better to refrain, believing that too much protein led to impure thoughts, which were a hindrance to their meditative spiritual lifestyle. Often, you will see a sign at the gates of temples saying, '不許葷酒入山門' – 'No garlic, other strong vegetables, meat, fish or alcohol is allowed to enter the temple gate'.

The prohibition was a mere policy statement for those leading religious lives, but it set the standard for the rest of society. It appears that non-religious Japanese people could not resist alcohol and fish, but drew the line at eating meat in their search for cleaner living.

In times of war and civil strife, such as in the Age of the Warring States, these prohibitions were loosened, and people hunted for game, mainly boar and deer. They had to eat them to survive. As soon as peace returned, people refrained from eating meat on the basis of social norm.

One of the side-effects of Japanese abstention from meat eating was physical. In the 250 years of peace under the Tokugawa shogunate, people's aversion to meat meant that the average height of the Japanese people decreased significantly. With the Meiji Restoration, the adoption of Western civilisation and, to a lesser degree, Western culture, eating meat became fashionable, and people quickly shrugged off their inhibitions. This means that, for the first time in their history, Japanese people have been eating meat on a continuous basis for 150 years. In the meantime, the average height of the Japanese people, both male and female, has increased by almost 20cm. Historically, we are the tallest Japanese.

By and large, meat-eating appears to have been good for us, although it may have been achieved at the expense of a meditative spiritual lifestyle.

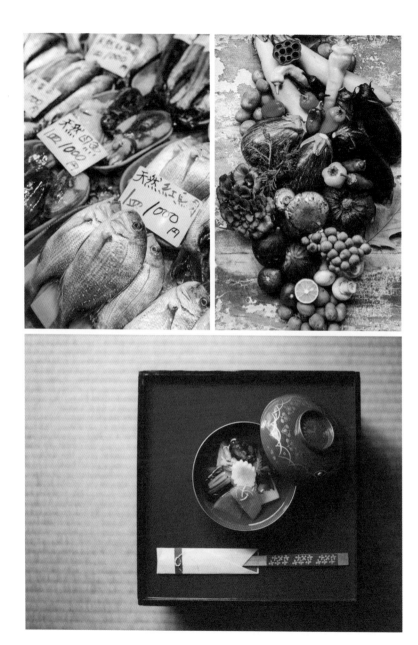

From fast food to main course

Tempura (天麩羅), that quintessentially Japanese deep-fried dish, actually has its origins in Portugal. The cooking method of deep-frying with a batter arrived in Japan in the 16th century with the Jesuits.

At the time, cooking oil was generally made from sesame seeds, and was so expensive that *tempura* was a food reserved for the rich. As the price of cooking oil came down with increased production during the Edo period, *tempura* became popular, particularly in the new capital, Edo, where it was sold by street vendors. It was one of three 'Edo foods' that originated and were popularised in Edo, alongside *sushi* and *soba* noodles.

Tempura as a street food was usually made with vegetables, especially root vegetables such as lotus root and sweet potato. Seafood such as shrimp and eel caught in Edo Bay was also used (and was known as *Edomae* [江戸前], meaning 'in front of Edo'). The ingredients were coated in a batter of egg and flour, then deep-fried in hot sesame oil in front of eager customers.

It was only much later, around the end of Tokugawa shogunate in the mid-19th century, that *tempura* vendors began to have their own restaurants. It wasn't until at least 1923 that *tempura* spread beyond the city now called Tokyo, when the Great Kantō earthquake destroyed the restaurants of many *tempura* chefs, who moved to Osaka and elsewhere to sell their food.

If you go to a specialist *tempura* restaurant in Tokyo you choose from the ingredients on display and tell the *tempura* chef behind the counter which ingredients you want to be fried. The knack of the chef is to control the oil's temperature in accordance with the ingredients so the *tempura* is fried with the core of the ingredients remaining soft and flavourful.

As mentioned above, *sushi* (鮨) also originates from Edo. However, a wider definition of *sushi* as a method of preserving fish with rice using vinegar existed long before that. What happened in Edo was the invention of *nigiri sushi* (握り寿司), where a piece of fish is served on top of a vinegar-flavoured rice ball. In other words, *sushi* as it is globally known today.

Unlike *tempura*, *sushi* only became popular in Edo in, it is generally believed, the first half of the 19th century, but it quickly caught on. At first, the rice portion of *sushi* was much bigger than it is today, and it was regarded as a quick snack, or even fast food.

The availability of fresh *Edomae* seafood was the important factor in the early days of *nigiri sushi*. As improved refrigeration techniques arrived, the ingredients used for *sushi* became more numerous. At first, they were almost exclusively the types of fish that could be caught in nearby seas, such as horse mackerel, sardine and bonito. Modern staples, such as tuna, came more recently as they became easier to transport and store.

    Sushi, like *tempura*, developed into a main-course meal served at restaurants through the efforts of chefs who were eager for a value-added business model. This resulted in more fashionable *sushi* restaurants that charge exorbitant prices for what is essentially a simple food that started life as a snack. Cynics complain about this inflationary phenomenon, but one must admit that there is something deeply alluring and Japanese about the minimalist charm of *sushi* and *sushi* restaurants that loosen our wallets.

Foreign foods gone native

One of the benefits of not having a world-beating cuisine of its own is that the Japanese have adopted many foreign foods as their own. *Tempura,* as mentioned previously, is a chief example, having been introduced to Japan by the Portuguese. Here are some other Japanese foods that actually came from further afield.

RAMEN (拉麺) Now regarded as one of Japan's major culinary exports, *ramen* actually originated in China. When Japanese soldiers returned from China after the Second World War, many brought with them recipes for Chinese noodles. One of those was for *ramen,* noodles made from flour and brine.

TONKATSU (豚カツ) This deep-fried pork fillet was introduced at the end of the 19th century and made popular by a restaurant in Tokyo's Ginza district, called Renga-tei (煉瓦亭). Its roots are distinctly European: French *côtelette,* Milanese *cotoletta* and German *schnitzel.*

AN-PAN (あんパン) Bread (*pan,* from the French *pain*) with a sweet filling made from red bean paste. Yasubei Kimura (木村安兵衛 1817–1889), a pioneering baker, was trying to popularise bread in Japan. In 1874, he came up with the idea of putting *anko* (あんこ), a sweet red bean paste and staple of Japanese confectionery, inside bread. It became a sensation when the Meiji emperor gave the bakery an imperial warrant. That bakery, Kimuraya, is still in Ginza and still hugely popular.

CASTELLA (カステラ) A sponge cake made from flour, sugar and eggs that was brought to Japan with the Jesuits in the 16th century. The name *castella* is a bit of mystery. Some say it comes from the Spanish region of Castilla, while others say it is derived from the Portuguese word for castle, *castelo.* There are *castella* bakeries in Nagasaki whose history goes back to the 17th century.

CURRY RICE (カレーライス) Japanese curry is nothing like any dish from India. Curry was introduced to Japan around 1873, taken from British naval recipes (thick, stew-like dishes) and served in the Imperial Japanese Navy. By the beginning of the 20th century, curry became popular and continues to be a family staple.

Why we have so many Michelin stars

Apparently, the American chef Anthony Bourdain could not get enough of Japan as a foodie destination – and not just for Japanese cuisine. Tokyo continues to boast more Michelin stars than any other city in the world.

Historically, the Japanese have been a modest bunch when it comes to eating. As discussed previously, we had been long under the Buddhist influence of avoiding meat, and the sumptuousness of a table was something to avoid, in line with the stoic virtues of samurai ethics.

In the immediate aftermath of the Second World War, the whole population of Japan was starving. The Japanese emerged from this dire situation in the 1950s, but food remained as an obsession in our collective psyche. Being a gourmet was once thought to be vulgar but now became a legitimate pursuit. Everybody became a food critic, and nothing contributes more to a standard of cooking than discerning foodies.

From the supply side, Japanese artisanal tradition seeped into the food industry. There had always been a tradition of master and apprentice in conventional Japanese cuisine, but it spread to all other food categories. Aspiring chefs competed to work as apprentices to top chefs, and then sought further training in France, Italy and other motherlands of their chosen cuisine. After a few years of overseas training, they returned to Japan to open their own restaurants and became new 'masters' in their own right to foster the next generation.

The size and growth of Tokyo as a megalopolis also helped these new restaurant owners. In places like Hong Kong, with limited size and concentration of real estate, landlords hike up rents as soon as a tenant restaurant becomes successful. As a result, customers are paying more for the rent than the food whereas Tokyo is kinder to start-up chefs in that respect. There have been a few big restaurant franchises trying to disrupt the cycle with slick interiors and the efficiency of centralised food production. Nevertheless, Japanese foodies tend to prefer smaller establishments with owner-chefs firmly in charge of operations.

All in all, we now have an ideal ecosystem in Japan for high-quality eateries to thrive. The media, from TV to publishing, ceaselessly streams information to fuel competition. It seems that Michelin stars will continue to shine above Tokyo for the foreseeable future.

Japanese whisky

The story of how whisky arrived in Japan is a well-known one in the country. Masataka Taketsuru (竹鶴政孝 1894–1979) went to Glasgow in 1918 to study chemistry, and later apprenticed with several Scottish distilleries. He returned to Japan with his Scottish wife Rita and started to produce whisky with a company that is now known as Suntory. He later started his own company, Nikka. Whiskies produced by both Suntory and Nikka are now regarded as being among the best in the world.

The problem with the whisky business is that you cannot immediately increase production, even if your product becomes popular. Higher production only materialises in more output a decade or so down the line. It requires patience and humility.

It was lucky for Japanese whisky that its pioneer distillers had these qualities in abundance. They knew they were attempting something difficult, and respected the original whisky makers of Scotland and their traditions. The quality we see in Japanese whiskies today owes much to this.

Drinking highly alcoholic spirits was not a Japanese habit and people were slow to take to whisky drinking. When the quality of other alcohol beverages plummeted in the poverty of the post-war period, whisky makers saw their chance, and the popularity of the beverage grew alongside a recovering Japan.

In a way, Japanese whiskies are now at a crossroads. The quality of the product and the producers' diligence have led, over a period of time, to success that has coincided with the emergence of Japan as an economic power. They are now in soul-searching mode to ensure their continuing success. As an example, after Suntory's *Hibiki* blended whisky won a prestigious prize, it became difficult to find. In response, Suntory made the bottles smaller. The move was condemned by the world's whisky aficionados as a quick money-making scheme.

The new situation poses a challenge for Japanese whisky makers, not just to maintain the high quality they have achieved, but to nurture their brands. That requires more than just humility, but a lot of patience and self-control.

Robatayaki and teppanyaki

Japanese communal eating habits have been a tame affair. We were light years behind the Chinese in sumptuousness – while an emperor in China could command all the delicacies under the sun to be assembled at his table, the Japanese had to make do with locally available ingredients.

Japanese dining style has been influenced by the tea ceremony, which was, in turn, influenced by Zen Buddhism and its tradition of *shōjin ryōri* (精進料理), meaning 'devotional cuisine'. Zen monks eat sparingly, barely enough to sustain themselves in their contemplative lifestyle. It is not so much feasting as dining on rations. It is certainly healthy, if far from fun.

All this means is that communal eating as entertainment came into the Japanese consciousness rather late. *Robatayaki* (炉端焼き) is a style of dining where food, usually fish, shellfish and vegetables, is slow-grilled on skewers over an open charcoal fire in front of diners, rather like a barbeque. It is modelled on the country lifestyle, where family members gather around a hearth to eat by the fireside. The style originated at a restaurant in Sendai in the 1950s.

Teppanyaki (鉄板焼き) is a method where food is grilled on a hot iron plate, also in front of diners. This style was made popular by a steakhouse in Kobe right after the war, and became a hit in the USA with the Benihana restaurant chain founded by Japanese entrepreneur Hiroaki 'Rocky' Aoki (青木廣彰) in the 1960s. It was re-imported to Japan following its success Stateside.

Both *robatayaki* and *teppanyaki* introduced showmanship and, consequently, fun into the Japanese dining experience.

It is telling that both styles were born in the period right after the war, when the Japanese were emerging from the chronic shortage of food. With the memory and fear of starvation receding, people took to eating as an easy way of appreciating the return of peace and enjoying the fruits of modest prosperity. As a result, we have added a new page to our culinary culture.

Life Outside

How to hike like a Japanese Emperor

If horse racing is the sport of British kings, then Japan's royal sport must surely be hiking.

Kunimi (国見), literally meaning 'looking at the kingdom', was a tradition in ancient Japan. On certain auspicious days, rulers went to the highest points of their domains to look over the lands they ruled by way of giving blessings for good harvests, and so on.

Naruhito, the Emperor of Japan (今上天皇徳仁) has taken *kunimi* to new heights. He is an avid hiker, and since the age of five, has climbed about 170 peaks throughout Japan. However, with or without this endorsement, hiking is a popular pursuit. There are several good mountains within easy reach of Tokyo, and even famous peaks above the 2,000m mark are no further than a day's journey away via well-connected train and local bus services.

Apart from the ancient practice of *kunimi*, mountain climbing has been historically linked with religious training. Some monks commit themselves to 100 or 1,000 days of continuous climbing of holy peaks as part of their devotion and search for Nirvana. Religious hermits in mountains known as *yamabushi* (山伏) are also following a religious tradition in which people don the *yamabushi*'s particular clothing and stay in the mountains, bearing the hardship of living outdoors and being exposed to the elements as physical training for religious purposes. Even now, ordinary people take part in *yamabushi* experiences for a limited period as a hobby or lifestyle choice.

Mainstream hikers are a more easy-going bunch. Nevertheless, they share their enthusiasm with those ancient traditions, going to the mountains to escape the busyness of their daily lives. The clean, fresh air of mountain forests is sufficient reward. *Shinrin-yoku* (森林浴) is the term the Japanese created for it, literally meaning 'forest bathing'. They say that 'bathing' in the fresh air of forests has positive physical effects. Nobody could argue against that.

Sumo: in praise of the big men

These days, sumo (相撲) is in limbo. It cannot make up its mind whether it is a sport or cultural event steeped in tradition. Like any other wrestling-type sports found all over the world, sumo's history goes back to the mythical age. In the Shinto religion, the sun goddess Amaterasu's people came to a Japan that was already populated by indigenous gods. Takemikazuchi, one of Amaterasu's newcomers, challenged the indigenous god Takeminakata to a bout of sumo. The former overwhelmed the latter, who fled to the province of Shinano and died from the wounds sustained in the bout. Takeminakata became the god of the Suwa Shrine (諏訪神社), which still thrives.

During the period in which the emperors ruled Japan, sumo tournaments became a form of entertainment and an event in the court calendar. An emperor actively looked for big, strong men throughout Japan to serve as professional sumo wrestlers, and an annual tournament was held in summer in front of him. It is thought that such sumo tournaments were dedicated to gods as prayers for good harvest.

As the power of emperors and their courts declined, so did sumo as a ceremonial spectacle. It survived as a recreational activity, but professional sumo wrestlers found it difficult to make a living after traditional sponsors and organisers of tournaments had left the scene. Oda Nobunaga (織田信長1534–1582), a famous warlord from the Age of the Warring States, emerged as sumo's saviour. He was already a big fan, and introduced rules and a structure of his own.

Under the peace guaranteed by the Tokugawa shogunate, popular culture flourished, and sumo became entertainment for the masses. Professional sumo wrestlers were once more in demand and the promoters of tournaments were keen to give events proper pomp and circumstance. A ranking system was introduced, with titles we recognise today, such as yokozuna (横綱), or 'grand champions'.

Professional sumo organisers began to add more pageantry and splendour to their tournaments with referees starting to wear more anachronistic costumes. The promotion of sumo wrestlers, especially to the top rank of yokozuna, is an archaic affair decided by a committee made up of the selected 'great and good' members of the Japanese establishment. Increasingly, sumo has become less like a sport and more like a collection of traditions which are, in reality, of modern origin.

Recently, *sumo* wrestlers have begun to get bigger meaning bouts are often won by the largest competitor, with little room for skilful wrestlers to shine. There has also been a decline in home-grown talent, and many top-class participants now come from Mongolia. Fifteen-day tournaments six times a year, which became standard in 1949, are taking their physical toll on the wrestlers. There are persistent rumours of bout-fixing among wrestlers to save their rankings and their bodies.

In short, professional *sumo* is in a bit of a quandary in this modern context. So many elements are screaming for reform and improvement but it is hindered by anachronistic tendencies to maintain the cultural traditions. There seems to be no easy answer.

Let's go to Kyoto

JR Tōkai (JR東海) is one of the Japanese railway companies and runs the *Shinkansen* 'bullet train' service between Tokyo and Kyoto. In 1993, it ran an ad campaign promoting the former capital city with the catchphrase, 'Yes, let's go to Kyoto'. It was so successful that the same catchphrase continues to this day, prompting lots of holidaymakers to jump on the super-fast train to satisfy their wanderlust.

When the bullet train was being developed in the early 1960s, the World Bank loaned US$80 million for the project. There was scepticism that train services dedicated only to passenger transport would be successful. Such pessimism was proved wrong. In its first year operating between Tokyo and Osaka, the bullet train carried an average of 84,000 passengers per day, which rose rapidly to around 231,000 passengers per day in its fifth year.

The reason why tourism is such a big part of leisure time in Japan is, in my opinion, because our lifestyle is very sedate and confined. Back when agriculture was the country's main industry, work in the fields required labourers' constant attention. People were tied to their land and had little time to venture outside their small villages. Even with the emergence of commercial activities and the rise in urban population, mostly in the Edo period, workers had no weekend respite as we know it today. Holidays were restricted to a few days in summer for *Obon* (お盆) to commemorate ancestors, and between three and seven days to celebrate the new year. Under such claustrophobic restrictions, people yearned to travel as an escape from everyday life.

In the Edo period, the most popular destination for those fortunate enough to have both leave and the necessary funds was the Ise Grand Shrine (伊勢神宮) dedicated to the goddess Amaterasu. It took about two weeks on foot (horses were not available to commoners) to get from Edo to Ise, and then on to Kyoto. The Tōkaidō coastal route had (and still does have) amazing views, particularly of Mt Fuji, as well as hostel towns known for their seafood dotted along the route.

People needed to roam. The destination itself had only a nominal purpose. It was the journey that mattered, as an escape from the reality of life at home. These factors remain true today. People needing a short break from reality take a weekend holiday and Kyoto is a good destination. It is convenient and there is always something to see.

Onsen

With its volcanic geography, Japan has many hot springs where the groundwater, warmed by geothermal heat, emerges to the surface. With their warmth and mineral content, hot springs have long been valued for their therapeutic benefits, and resort facilities, from simple bed-and-breakfasts to full scale entertainment developments, have flourished around each of them. They are known as *onsen* (温泉), which simply means 'hot springs'.

Onsen as a term is defined by law. In 1948, the *onsenhou*, or Hot Spring Law, was enacted for the protection of hot springs and their safe usage (the prevention of natural gas explosions is a big issue). For a hot spring to be officially recognised, the water must be above a certain temperature at the source, and it must contain minerals or other matter above a certain level.

There are more than 3,000 *onsen* with accommodation facilities throughout Japan, from the northern tip of Hokkaido to the southern islands of Okinawa. Some are better known than others, perhaps for their geographical proximity to traditional centres of population. Arima *Onsen* (有馬温泉) near Kobe is one of the oldest recorded. It has undoubtedly benefitted from being close to Kyoto and Osaka. Similarly, *onsen* around the Hakone (箱根) area in Kanagawa prefecture became well-known due to the proximity to Edo (later Tokyo), and for being on the roadside of the Tōkaidō route between Edo and Kyoto.

Other *onsen* are known for their therapeutic values. Kusatsu *Onsen* (草津温泉) in Gunma prefecture is deep in the mountains and hard to get to. Nevertheless, it has been one of the most popular and famous resorts for centuries, as its hot water, rich in sulphur, was believed to cure or at least ease the symptoms of diseases including syphilis and leprosy.

You didn't have to be sick to enjoy *onsen*, of course. They have been popular tourist destinations ever since tourism took off in the 19th century, and continue to attract weekend travellers.

Volcanoes and earthquakes are facts of life in Japan. Under the circumstances, *onsen* are some of the best compensation that nature could have given the Japanese people. We can stop worrying about the earth moving under our feet as we enjoy a good soak in hot water from the earth's natural boiler room.

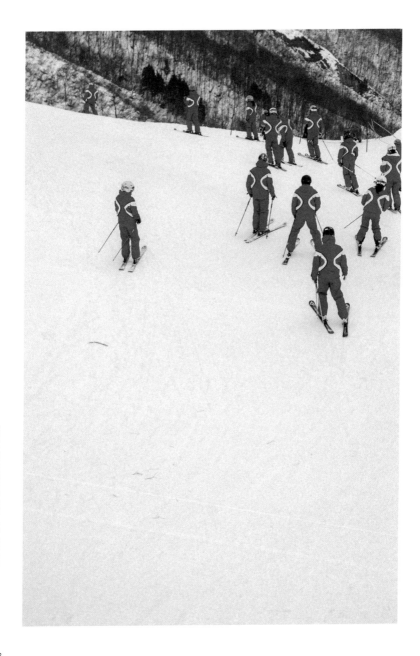

Take Me Out to the Snowland

In 1987, a run-of-the-mill romantic comedy film about a young couple which played out against the backdrop of ski resorts was released. That film, *Take Me Out to the Snowland* (私をスキーに連れてって), went on to become a monster hit.

In the late 80s, Japan was riding high on the heady wave of the bubble economy. The younger generation had cash in their hands, but few ideas about how to spend it. Skiing was becoming popular, but this film pushed it into the mainstream and everybody started to flock to the pistes.

While poor resort infrastructure and chronic underinvestment saw queues at the chairlifts and waiting times of an hour or more, it was nevertheless 'cool' for young Japanese to be seen to be skiing. The well-known Prince Hotels group was one of the major developers of Japan's ski resorts, and still operates many of them today.

However, as the economy bubble burst, skiing holidays were among the first of the luxuries that one could do without in times of austerity. In 1993, there were about 18 million skiers in Japan. By 2013, that was down to around 8 million.

As the Chinese economy started to roar, those who had made money from the Japanese skiing boom in the 80s and 90s pinned their hopes on their large neighbour, confident that they were on the up again. The Chinese skiing boom wasn't as universal as they might have hoped, but a sizeable number of the newly minted wealthy took up the sport, preferring to go to Japan for their new hobby.

Japan is currently going through its second ski boom, but it is very different from the first. The big difference is what the Japanese tourism industry calls 'the inbounds' – Australians and Chinese who come to enjoy 'Japow', also known as Japanese powder snow. They are seeking top-class resort infrastructure to match their high expectations, not the one hour-plus waiting times of yore. The early adapters to their demands, such as Niseko (ニセコ町) in Hokkaido, or Nozawaonsen (野沢温泉) and Hakuba (白馬村) in Nagano, are emerging as the winners.

How to fish

Fishing is a big deal in Japan. There are some 7 million anglers, and the pastime has a long tradition. As urbanisation gathered pace, and the population started to be concentrated in big cities such as Tokyo and Osaka, fishing became a hobby for city dwellers, bringing them into the great outdoors.

In the 60s and 70s, catching fish was the paramount purpose of fishing. If this strikes you as rather obvious, you are obviously not a fishing type. While anglers competed to catch more fish, rivers and coastal waters suffered a decline in stocks. To sustain fragile rural economies dependent on anglers, local governments, as well as fishery and leisure industry groups, started to replenish stocks by releasing farmed fish into the water, especially in freshwater fishing areas. Some anglers also secretly introduced foreign species, such as bluegill and black bass, which are prized for their strength. These short-term, short-sighted interventions had serious negative effects on the ecosystem. Ultimately, if slowly, the environmental impact was recognised, and fishing manners expected of 21st-century anglers were adopted. Nowadays, catch-and-release is the norm.

Japanese fishing is perhaps notable for its variety of methods. While the size of catch still matters, the fishing method is a matter of pride for an angler. The harder a method used to catch fish, the more respect an angler commands.

Tenkara fly-fishing (テンカラ), where a fly is attached to a fixed length of line, is a popular Japanese way of angling. Lure fishing, where casting does not require a wide and open space, is also popular, and there are always lively discussions as to the types of lures to be used for particular fish and fishing points. More exotic Japanese fishing methods include ayu (アユ) fishing, where a live sweetfish is used as bait. Sweetfish are very territorial, so if one sees another in its territory, the sweetfish attacks and is then caught by the hook that is attached to the live bait. The skills of navigating the sweetfish underwater take years to master, and competition among these anglers is fierce.

Perhaps the most unique Japanese method is *tanago* fishing (タナゴ釣り). A *tanago* is a type of carp that only grows to about 6–10cm and lives in rice paddies and their irrigation systems. To fish them, you use a miniature rod and tackle with a minute hook. Aficionados claim that using small gear with delicate skills to catch a tiny fish is proportionally equal to catching a whale using a large harpoon in terms of excitement. It is, of course, all in the mind of the angler. Like seeing a lush forest in a bonsai tree, it is almost Zen-like.

People of the mountains

Japan is 70 percent mountain, so it's no surprise that the sustenance from the bounty provided by mountains and the endless temperate rainforest that covered large areas was vital for indigenous peoples such as the *Jōmon* (縄文人), whose period lasted for some 14,000 years.

The mountain people eventually retreated eastwards and northwards, where the climate and geography made rice-growing more difficult, but some remained in the peaks. The mountains became a sanctuary, and a forbidden area for those who lived on the plains. Skip forward in time, and this forbiddance became associated with holiness. As the Japanese economy advanced, it needed the expertise of the mountain dwellers. All the magnificent wooden structures, those ancient temples or shrines we see around Japan, required the skills of expert woodcutters. Only they knew how to trek across the mountains to reach the desired trees, cut them down and carry them downstream for use on various building sites.

The ability of the mountain people to be able to crisscross seemingly impenetrable mountains and survive harsh conditions became a source of awe among the 'flatlanders' and this led to numerous folklore tales based on their mystery. There are numerous stories of *oni* (鬼), troll-like people who usually come down from the mountains or from hidden conclaves deep in the mountains to play mischief among the farmers. The word *oni* is believed to have derived from the term for 'big men'.

With the introduction of Western civilisation and the industrialisation of Japan from the mid-19th century, the number of mountain people, known as *sanka* (山窩), had dwindled. Urbanisation and the availability of work in the city lured them away from the mountains. The post-war economic recovery and mechanisation of the forestry industry finally lured the last of the mountain people out of their ancestral habitat and into the cities.

However, there are still those who believe in the mountain people living in pockets hidden deep in the Japanese mountains, and their legacy lives on through the rich tradition of woodcrafts they created.

Life Inside

Go: Japanese Wimbledon

Igo (囲碁), or simply *go* (碁), is a board game believed to have been invented in China more than 2,500 years ago. Two players take turns to place a 'stone' – either black or white – on an intersection on a 19 x 19 grid. Each intersection of the grid counts as a piece of territory, and both players compete to surround more territories with their stones. Stones may be captured if they are isolated and surrounded by the opponent.

The rules of *go* are simple, but the game is complex, and tactical as well as strategic. While IBM's Deep Blue computer beat grandmaster Garry Kasparov at chess in 1996, it took until 2015 for Google DeepMind's AlphaGo program to beat a human at *go*.

Go arrived in Japan around the 7th century, from China via Korea, and became popular amongst aristocrats. In the 14th and 15th centuries, it spread across class divides and professional players appeared. They were hired by the rich and powerful as teachers, and became members of their entourages. In the peacetime of the Edo period, the Tokugawa shogunate offered patronage to master players, and ordinary people started *go* clubs to compete and study the game's tactics.

Currently, Japan has about 2.5 million *go* players and worldwide, there are about 40 million. Japan had the advantage of professionalising *go* earlier than other countries, so it dominated championship titles during most of the 20th century. Since the late 1980s, international tournaments such as the LG Cup and the Asian TV Cup have been held mostly in East Asia. After a short spell of Japanese dominance, Chinese and Korean masters have become dominant.

In reality, *go* has become an international game in which the 'Big Three' of Japan, China and Korea are locked in a continuous battle for top place. I believe it is a healthy thing. We celebrate our common heritage and the mutual recognition of excellence in the players representing each nation.

Shōgi: Japanese chess

Like any other variation of chess worldwide, Japan's shōgi (将棋) is believed to go all the way back to India's ancient game of *chaturanga*. That game became *xiangqi* in China and *janggi* in Korea.

It is not clear when these variations of chess arrived in Japan, but it is believed to have been around the same time as the game *go*. The chess-type games would have differed in complexity, as any form of chess involves complicated rules with different types of playing pieces. Those earlier versions featured exotic (for the Japanese) pieces such as elephants and tigers.

By the 17th century, the game had simplified itself, become uniform, had rules, and developed into something similar to the present-day game of *shōgi*. At the same time, the concept of *mochigoma* (持ち駒) was incorporated into the game. Under this uniquely Japanese rule, a piece captured from an opponent can be reused by the opposite player and deployed at any time, and on any spot, on the board. This adds another level of complexity to the game.

Like *go*, *shōgi* enjoyed patronage from the Tokugawa shogunate and became popular across all classes. The Meiji Restoration also meant that both games lost such patronage. In 1924, professional *shōgi* players organised themselves into what was to become the Japan Shōgi Association.

Unlike *go*, *shōgi* is unique to Japan, and there is little interaction with overseas players. Nevertheless, *shōgi* has about five million players, more than *go* in Japan. While *go* is, at first sight, geometrically mysterious and wears an air of complexity, *shōgi* has direct visual appeal and the game is more combative. There are many tales of famous matches between master players of old, as well as new. There have been popular songs, TV dramas, films and even manga comic book stories written about *shōgi* players, ensuring more fans and a continued supply of future master players.

Martial arts

Martial arts did not take off in Japan until the peace of the Tokugawa shogunate around 300 years ago. Before that, people did not practise martial arts – real life provided ample opportunity for those willing to try their martial prowess with inevitably fatal consequences for some.

During the Tokugawa shogunate, samurai became hereditary civil servants whose job was to carry out civil administrative work for the shogun or their feudal lords. Nevertheless, samurai had to maintain the semblance of being a warrior breed to maintain their social status. Various schools of swordsmanship (*kendō* 剣道 – 'the way of the sword') evolved. Skilled practitioners found gainful employment as sword masters throughout Japan.

Kendo became even more popular with the invention of the *shinai* (竹刀), a practice sword made from torn bamboo tied together. Previously, *kendo* was practised with a wooden sword, which meant it was a lethal blunt weapon. Fighting with one, even for training purposes, was a dangerous affair. A *shinai*, on the other hand, was softer, and allowed participants to engage in mock fighting quite safely. It also introduced the element of sport and competition to *kendo*.

Judo (柔道) was established by Jigorō Kanō (嘉納治五郎 1860–1938). He came from a wealthy merchant family in the Kobe area which was known for shipping and making *sake*. *Jujutsu* (柔術), the martial art of close combat without weapons, had been practised as part of wider martial arts, but Kanō gave it a structure, rules of competition, and made it into a sport that is practiced all over the world.

Karate (空手) literally means 'empty hand'. It actually originates from the school of Chinese martial arts like *kung fu*, and developed in Okinawa. It was introduced to mainland Japan at the turn of the 20th century and quickly became popular.

Thanks to the Japanese martial tradition and the respect with which people held the mastery of these arts and sport in general, martial artists enjoyed fame and a decent living. The tradition extends to modern-day variants of martial arts, such as Ultimate Fighting. Participants are generally respected by fans in Japan, who see them as masters rather than entertainers. You can find *dōjō* (道場), or gyms, for *kendo*, *judo* and *karate* in every corner of Japan.

Japanese jazz

With the end of the Second World War came the Americans. With them came their barracks, and soldiers needed recreation and entertainment – music. Luckily, all the former musicians from the now disbanded Japanese military bands were looking for gainful employment. They were quickly marshalled to relatively lucrative engagements at the 'clubs' for those American barracks, where they learned to play a new kind of music called 'jazz'.

The military clubs were off limits to ordinary Japanese people, except for the musicians. However, that didn't stop the music seeping out of the clubs and finding its way into Japanese homes. Reconstruction work gathered pace to the sound of jazz and its syncopated and swinging rhythms. In those days, Western popular music was all called 'jazz' in Japan.

While the American military took the lead in beginning desegregation after the Korean War, American society was heading for the turmoil of the civil rights movement in the sixties. Around this period, the musician Art Blakey was making decidedly 'black' jazz with his band, the Jazz Messengers, which the critics called 'hard bop'. Blakey's music reached Japan via France, where it was featured in their *New Wave* films, and became huge hits – particularly his classic, *Moanin'*. Hearing of his popularity in Japan, Blakey toured the country with his band for the first time in 1960.

Upon arrival, Blakey was surrounded by enthusiastic fans. He was asked by one if he could be in a photo with him. 'But I'm black,' said the star. The fan replied, 'But, of course!'. Blakey instantly fell in love with Japan, and toured with the Jazz Messengers almost every year until his death in 1990.

Jazz is not the most popular form of music in Japan these days, but it still has a strong and faithful following. When the popularity of jazz was on the wane in the US, Japanese fans and record labels provided American musicians with steady support. Japanese jazz musicians are also thriving, and there are live jazz houses in every major city.

Jazz was perhaps the best gift that the American occupation brought to Japan in the turmoil of the post-war period.

From Kurosawa to Studio Ghibli

The biggest tragedy to befall Japanese cinema was the Second World War. When film as an art form was reaching its zenith globally, Japanese film was appropriated by warmongers as a propaganda tool. This loss of creative freedom asphyxiated Japanese film-making.

After the war, film was the king of popular entertainment. So many were made, but few have survived the test of time. *Seven Samurai* (七人の侍), the masterpiece of director Akira Kurosawa (黒澤明 1910–1998), and the calling card for Japanese cinema, was one of about 50 Japanese films released in 1954.

One thing that strikes the Japanese about *Seven Samurai* and most of Kurosawa's other films is how 'Western' they appear. Kurosawa's hero was the American director John Ford. Consequently, the film is more universal in its appeal. However, it makes us a little uneasy that the story is not anchored to any geographical or historical facts that we Japanese are familiar with, and the film has a blunt feel about it. In that sense, Kurosawa's dramaturgy breaks from Japanese tradition and sensibilities.

More in keeping with Japanese tastes are the films of Yasujirō Ozu (小津安二郎 1903–1963), known mainly for *Tokyo Story* (which came out a year before *Seven Samurai*). Nothing much happens in Ozu's films in terms of action. His stories are observations of ordinary people's everyday lives. Even Ozu's famous technique of shooting from a low angle makes the viewer feel as if we are witnessing events as we sit on the floor together with the actors. It makes us feel at home.

Unfortunately, before Kurosawa, Ozu or any other film-makers could properly restart Japan's film industry, it went into decline. People stayed at home and watched television.

Japanese film came back onto the world stage with the animated films of Studio Ghibli in the 1990s. However, most of the studio's stories do not take place in Japan. Even the Oscar-winning *Spirited Away* (千と千尋の神隠し), while starting in an ordinary Japanese landscape, soon takes the viewer into a fantasy world.

Hikikomori

Since the 1990s, it has come to Japan's attention that there are a number of young people, mostly male, who refuse to interact with society. The issue was first raised when it was discovered that there were many students, mostly male, who refused to attend school. As time went on, their number swelled, and their average age increased.

According to statistics published in 2005, there were about 1.6 million people in Japan suffering from such social withdrawal. If you include those still managing to keep only minimum contact with the outside world, that number increased to more than 3 million people.

The word given to such people is *hikikomori* (引きこもり), meaning 'social withdrawal or isolation'. It applies roughly to those who refuse contact with society for more than six months or are diagnosed with various types of mental disorders affecting anxiety or adjustment, and so on.

When the BBC picked up this topic for a report in the 2000s, it attracted a sizeable response from British viewers who recognised similar symptoms in themselves or family members. Such mental disorders and their manifestation in a hermit-like lifestyle are not specific to modern Japanese society, but they cannot be isolated from the society in which they occur, because social intercourse is the core issue.

The homogeneity of Japanese society and its pressure to conform may make it difficult for those who feel 'left behind' to find a suitable place for themselves. The ready availability of a virtual society online also seems to encourage anti-social behaviour in the real world. Presence and personality are easier to manipulate on the internet than in the real world.

Although the symptoms of *hikikomori* were first discovered among young boys, we are now increasingly aware of – and alarmed by – its spread to the middle-aged and elderly, again mostly male. With the collapse of the convention of lifelong employment in Japan's corporate world, middle-aged workers forced to contemplate a career change in, say, their forties, can be vulnerable to a sudden onset of withdrawal. Elderly people in rural areas are also facing a change in their social landscape and are at risk of withdrawal.

It is tempting to dismiss those suffering from social withdrawal as weak-minded dropouts. However, one must remember that a society that takes care of its weak is stronger as a unit for its compassion. For a community-orientated society such as Japan, we ignore those who suffer at our own peril.

Family Life and Life's Milestones

Birth, Japanese style

It is rare for a Japanese child to be born to an unmarried couple. The Organisation for Economic Co-operation and Development (OECD) found that in 2014, only about 2.3 percent of babies were born out of wedlock in Japan. In the US, the figure was 40.2 percent, and 47.6 percent in the UK. Only Korea surpassed Japan in this respect, with just 1.9 percent of births outside marriage.

Childbirth in Japan is a cross-generational affair. Pregnant women tend to return to their parents' home when they are close to their due date. This practice is called *satogaeri* (里帰り), literally meaning to 'return home'. Women usually register with the hospital nearest their parents' house, and according to a survey in 2005, just over half of deliveries take place in hospital facilities.

About 50 percent of husbands now accompany their wives at the birth, a 2011 survey found. This number increases with younger couples. Doctors are encouraging fathers to be present, and their recommendations seem to be heeded.

New Japanese mothers and their babies tend to stay longer in hospital than their overseas counterparts. A week seems to be the usual maximum, whereas in the US, mothers are encouraged to stay only overnight after the birth.

Japanese women tend to return to their parents' homes with their babies to recuperate, another tradition that comes from a time when a mother's health after the ordeal of childbirth was far from secure. The word *tokoage* (床上げ), literally meaning 'to tidy up the futon', means that a mother is strong enough to return to her normal duties – as well as caring for the baby by herself.

These outdated traditions also extend to facilitating fathers to remain at work right up to the birth of their child, and return immediately afterwards. They are expected, as a matter of course, to be estranged from their wives and babies for a period.

A widely known statistic is that Japan's birth rate has remained below 2 (less than the replacement value for the parents) for nearly half a century, contributing to the decline in its population and resulting in a rapidly aging society. While the active support provided by maternal grandparents is a nice way of bringing families together, it somehow works to exclude active participation from a husband's parents. The Japanese government is actively encouraging companies to adopt paid paternity leave, but social norms based on tradition and workplace pressures are preventing men from taking full advantage of this. By taking cross-generational support for granted, Japanese society is making it more difficult than necessary for women to have babies and enjoy motherhood by choice. It is estimated that about 20 percent of pregnancies end in an abortion as a parental choice, as opposed to a termination for health issues for either a woman or her foetus.

With the serious population downturn already underway, Japanese government and society are both keenly aware of the need to change their attitudes towards childbirth. The reality, however, is changing very slowly. Given that childbirth is increasingly becoming just a once-in-a-lifetime event for most young parents, they still look to their own parents for advice, with their values and norms from a bygone era. And there are more of them around than babies these days.

How to beat the Japanese school system

Compared to East Asian countries like China and Korea, Japan was not fanatical about education in the past. Nevertheless, the peace that ensued under the Tokugawa shogunate promoted commerce and encouraged the whole population to become literate. This was achieved by the prevalence of private tutors (often Buddhist monks and out-of-service samurai) teaching local children at *terakoya* (寺子屋), little shacks in a temple. The basic subjects were *yomi-kaki-soroban* (読み書き算盤), or reading, writing and abacus (basic arithmetic).

All these private arrangements became industrialised with the Meiji Restoration. To have your children educated became a duty under the constitution, and is still a part of the new constitution of 1946. A massive education boom began, fuelled by a bestselling book called *An Encouragement of Learning* (学問のすすめ) published in 1872 by scholar and educationalist Fukuzawa Yukichi (福澤諭吉), who is also the current Mr 10,000-yen note.

Today, competition to get into a good school can be fierce. At each level, there are entrance examinations. Paradoxically, the fierceness of competition is fanned by parents' wish to avoid such exams. The aforementioned Fukuzawa founded a private university, Keiō Gijuku Daigaku, which has affiliated primary schools. Once you are at a Keiō primary school, you don't need to take entrance exams to progress through Keiō's middle school, Keiō's high school and, ultimately, Keiō University. Consequently, high-minded competitive parents send their toddlers to cram schools to prepare them for the entrance exams for primary schools.

While competition for the best schools remains fierce, the Japanese educational system is also experiencing a shrinking young population. At the not-so-top-notch end of the scale, schools are struggling to fill their classrooms. Recently, many educational establishments have introduced a system where applicant students are selected for admission on the basis of their school records and other achievements, rather than *pro forma* entrance examinations.

Those who survive this tortuous road tend to look down on the private education route and go on to occupy the higher echelons of Japanese society. But they are also doomed forever to search for the right answers and the perfect test scores in a world where the right answers are not immediately obvious.

How the Japanese fall in love

Love may be timeless and universal, but courtship follows fashion. The Japanese courtship style has varied over history and geography. As I have already mentioned, aristocrats in the Heian period led a polygamous lifestyle, in which men called on each of their wives and any children were brought up by their mothers (see page 55). In the east of Japan, where samurai thrived, family was a tighter unit by necessity. With on-going neighbourly feuds and shifting alliances, men had no time for cruising around the countryside from one wife to another, like a bee pollinating flowers. There, monogamy was the norm and wives had more powerful agency in family affairs.

Romance has taken many forms in Japan, as it often does. However, with the sudden onset of modern society under the Meiji Restoration, the Japanese collectively experienced a sudden social upheaval which produced a disconnect in our tradition, and we had to grapple with the question of what should be the new norm for love and romance – which ultimately lead to the question of how a family should be formed in modern Japan. This goes some way to explaining the heaps of boring romantic novels that were written in the last 150 years or so in Japan, few of which have withstood the test of time. We have not yet had our Jane Austen or Brontë sisters.

In the late 80s, Japanese TV produced what is called *torendi dorama* (トレンディドラマ), or 'Trendy Dramas'. They were essentially romantic comedies set in Tokyo, and were wildly popular. Against the backdrop of big city life, where people are strangely lonely amongst all-engulfing crowds, the protagonists met their fated partners in seemingly unexpected ways. After overcoming run-of-the-mill difficulties (disapproving families, uncooperative friends, work demands), they lived happily ever after. They were banal in the extreme. Nevertheless, in a simple tale of boy-meets-girl, young viewers sought inspiration as well as affirmation of their own real love lives.

Japanese TV is still producing latter-day incarnations of the *torendi dorama*, but they are not commanding the popularity or influence they once enjoyed. It appears that single Japanese have finally come of age, and do not require a TV drama as reassurance. After all, you only have to meet one right person. There is no need for that special personal experience to conform to what is peddled as mass entertainment.

How to get married

Fewer people are getting married in Japan, and those who do wed are getting older. The latest available statistics show that about 5 in 1,000 people married in 2016, as opposed to more than 6 in 1,000 in 1996.

Still, marriage continues to be a life goal that many people are trying to achieve. It is just that society and modern lifestyles are making it somehow more difficult with added complications.

Japanese brains may be stressed from everyday life, but nature finds a way of bringing people together. About 25 percent of Japanese women getting married are pregnant, according to government statistics from 2010. In tropical Okinawa prefecture, the percentage goes up to more than 40 percent.

Pregnancy before marriage used to be frowned upon, but not so much now. With population decline a serious national issue, people have slowly become more benign towards a young couple with a little one soon to follow. Sadly, the same government statistics show that about 40 percent of such marriages end in divorce.

Marriage necessitates a wedding – a relatively recent custom in Japan. In the Heian period, aristocratic marriages were basically private coming-out parties for hitherto clandestine lovers. Between the 12th and 19th centuries, weddings among samurai families became more ornate, as the ceremony came to symbolise the alliance of two families. Customs such as an engagement ceremony, called a *yuinō* (結納), where the families of the bride and groom exchange gifts, developed gradually during this period, and were later copied by commoners. The actual wedding usually took place at the home of whichever family with whom the newlyweds were to live, and there was little religious tone to the ceremony.

Weddings as a celebration of a couple are a recent phenomenon. As such, modern Japanese people (well, mostly women) had a free hand in creating the new custom.

Weddings at a Shinto shrine became popular in 1900 after Emperor Taishō (大正天皇), then still a crown prince, married his wife in the Shinto shrine in the palace compound. This was the first time any religious organisation had been involved in people's matrimonial affairs in Japan.

Some modern Japanese brides-to-be aspired to a European style white wedding in a church due to their exposure to Western culture. However, many Christian churches insisted on religious conversion before the ceremony. Sensing a gap in the market, Japanese hotels and other commercial function venues started building mock chapels to offer 'Christian-style' weddings, which became very popular.

Not to be outdone, Buddhist temples tried to cut in on the action, but suffered from image issues as they were too associated with death and funerals.

Bentō box wars

The oft-cited argument for a school uniform is that it ensures equality among children by eliminating the element of futile fashion contests. Somehow, the same argument may need to be applied to food in Japanese schools.

Most public elementary and junior high schools provide school lunches, called *kyūshoku* (給食). Often, children take turns to serve the food to their classmates, so they learn not only about food, but to take pride and joy in serving others, be grateful for the meal, and to enjoy communal eating.

Kyūshoku has eased the pressure on parents by removing the daily need to pack a lunchbox, or *bentō* (弁当). *Bentō* are only needed for special occasions like school outings and picnics on school sports days, or *undōkai* (運動会).

To be sure, *bentō* is not just for school lunches. The word is used for any packed mobile meal. Adults enjoy *bentō* at, say, cherry-blossom viewing parties and other outings, and some famous restaurants are known for making *bentō* boxes fit for such occasions, with extravagant contents and aesthetically pleasing presentation.

Still, nobody expected the extravagance to hit *bentō* for school children. Somehow, around the 2000s, people started making children's *bentō* boxes depicting popular cartoon characters, cars or animals, using ingredients to draw and create the images. They are called *kyaraben* (キャラ弁), a word created from 'character' (as in characters from animation films) and *bentō*.

The emergence of blogs and social media fanned the boom, with an ever-increasing number of creators uploading photos of their opuses online for all to see, appreciate and emulate.

It is putting parents with less time on their hands (not to mention creativity or dexterity) under pressure in the never-ending battle for one-upmanship, but the boom shows no sign of abating. Probably because it is linked with that most Japanese of aesthetic values: *kawaii* (かわいい), or cuteness.

How to make a bentō box

1. **Think about the proportions.** Bentō boxes can be as elaborate as you want and may feature many items, but the three key ingredients are rice, fish or meat, and pickled vegetables. These are the foundation upon which any bentō box variations are built.

2. **Add flavour to your rice.** The main ingredient of any bentō box is rice. Unfortunately, rice does not hold its flavour particularly well when it gets cold. The easiest way to maintain cooked rice's delicate flavour is to add salt – which also acts as a preservative – or alternatively, try adding some sesame seeds. Other ways to improve the quality of your bentō box rice, include cooking it with other flavourful ingredients, such as bamboo shoots, diced octopus or clams.

3. **Keep your bentō balanced.** As part of a balanced diet, a bentō box should include a main source of protein. This can be fish, often grilled with salt (again, good for preservation), or meat cooked in such a way which keeps, such as roast beef. For a vegetarian bentō, you can try beans (edamame are good) or tofu as a protein source.

4. **Pickled vegetables** are usually inserted in a corner of the box, to complement the balanced diet, as well as to add colour and flavour. Sour and crunchy vegetables also help to satisfy the appetite.

5. **Think about appearance.** Remember that the aim with a bentō box is to create a meal that is as appealing to the eyes as to the taste buds. Colour is key to a visually exciting bentō box. Choose brightly coloured vegetables to contrast against the rice.

6. **Avoid excess liquid.** For ease of transporting, it is best to avoid watery foods or anything with a lot of sauce, as liquid may leak out. If you do want to include sauces or condiments, then use a separate container.

How to live to a hundred

While aging populations are a global phenomenon, Japan stands out from the crowd for its population's long life expectancy (about 84 years), the number of elderly (more than 33 million are over 65, about 26 percent of the Japanese population) and the speed at which the population is becoming aged (the number of the elderly has multiplied four times over the last 40 years).

The longevity of the Japanese, 86 for women and 80 for men, ranks second in the world to Hong Kong and is the envy of everywhere else. For the Japanese themselves, it is pleasing to be praised for what we achieve as a matter of habit, rather than as a result of strenuous effort.

The Japanese are sitting at a comfortable crossroads of both Western and Chinese medical traditions. We enjoy one of the best universal healthcare systems in line with what centuries of Western medical advances can provide. At the same time, the Japanese attitude towards health is deeply influenced by the Chinese thinking of yōjō (養生), or nurturing health through lifestyle. Attending to illness is the last resort.

The Japanese diet contributes hugely to the health of our nation in this respect. Nutritional balance has always been a part of our cuisine, even in the humblest of daily meals. Ichijūissai (一汁一菜) is the word to describe the most modest of meals, referring to one soup and one vegetable dish to go with a bowl of rice. A healthy appetite is praised as a product of hard labour, and gluttony is shunned as unseemly behaviour.

The weak links in an otherwise ideal diet are perhaps the reliance on rice and the use of too much salt. The Japanese are nevertheless aware of this. Metabo (メタボ), a Japanese–English term for metabolic deficiency, is currently a watchword for the health-conscious, and people are avoiding excess intake of carbohydrates. Faced with low demand for rice, producers are providing the market with healthier products such as zakkokumai (雑穀米), rice mixed with millet as an alternative to pure white rice. Too much salt seems to result in relatively high instances of stomach cancer among the Japanese; to go some way to combatting this, manufacturers are filling supermarket shelves with all sorts of products, from pickled vegetables to miso paste, labelled gen-en (減塩), or 'reduced salt'. The health food industry in Japan is happily led by health-conscious consumers.

Funerals

As a social display of decency for a deceased person's family, funerals are for the living. In Japan, death brings family together and reminds us of our Japanese-ness.

There is nothing like a funeral to encourage the building of consensus. Family members have to be notified to gather, even the estranged and feuding ones. There may be inevitable discord to follow over the inheritance, but procedures for a funeral ceremony must be agreed as a matter of urgency – usually within 24 hours of the deceased's passing, due to hygiene issues.

There is a wake before the day of funeral, called *otsuya* (お通夜). It literally means 'all night long'. In reality, it is a limited time (about two hours) in the evening, where people gather around the body, now properly cleaned and dressed by a professional, listen to a Buddhist monk reciting some mantra, then share a light meal, usually *sushi*, which is quick to order and easy to share, plus *sake*. The chief mourner, or *moshu* (喪主 – usually the deceased's spouse or the eldest child), is busy dealing with the guests, thanking them for their attendance despite the short notice and/or long distance. Other family members are also busy, wondering if they have ordered enough *sushi* and *sake* to go around.

On the day of the funeral, most of the *dramatis personae* return for the more elaborate Buddhist funeral rituals, including the monk and the guests, and anyone who could not make the previous night. The deceased's family members are now resigned to the fact that the bones will be heading for the family tomb in the monk's temple, and that the new generation of family members will have to keep paying a maintenance fee for it. The *moshu* continues to be busy, exercising the superhuman diplomatic skill of displaying an adequate amount of sorrow while trying to remember the names and faces of the deceased's extended network of friends and contacts. One good thing is that they bring a packet of condolence money, called *kōden* (香典) – literally, in a wonderful Japanese euphemism, 'incense money'. Apparently, ¥5,000 per person is the going rate. This would go only so far in easing the cost of the funeral, not to mention the tomb fee for the temple, but every little helps.

Both the wake and funeral ceremony may be held at the deceased's home. If there are space issues, the funeral services can rent out their hall, or the family temple would oblige.

After the ceremony, the coffin is moved to a specially made *reikyūsha* (霊柩車), or hearse, which is usually a black limousine with an elaborate Japanese roof design, to be carried to the local crematorium.

Most crematoria in Japan are run by the local government, except in Tokyo, where a private company has a monopoly. It is usual for family members to watch the coffin going into the furnace. This is the first moment when family members are finally allowed some private moments with the deceased and they cry.

The bones, whiter than you could ever imagine, come out of the furnace and all the family members are encouraged to pick them up with special chopsticks to put them into an urn. Finally, the crematorium attendant scoops the remaining bits and pieces into the urn, which is then sealed. You take the urn back home and make arrangements with the monk to put it in the family tomb at some future date.

Funerals have produced two major hit films. Director Jūzō Itami (伊丹 十三) released *Osōshiki* (お葬式 – *The Funeral*) in 1984, while Yōjirō Takita (滝田 洋二郎) won an Oscar for 2008's *Okuribito* (おくりびと – *Departures*).

Holidays and
Celebrations

January: New Year's Day

Oshōgatsu (お正月) is hugely important in Japan. We Japanese are baffled about why most of the West (with the notable exception of Scotland) ignores this most auspicious of days and treats it like a minor addition to Christmas.

One of the most important rituals for New Year's Day is a visit to the local shrine to pray for the Shinto gods' blessings for the forthcoming year. This observance is called *hatsumōde* (初詣), or 'the first visit to the shrine of the year'. Returning home, we eat a special meal called *osechi-ryōri* (御節料理), literally meaning 'the meal for a special occasion', but it invariably refers to New Year's Day. *Osechi-ryōri* is basically a bentō consisting of various foods with some connotation of good luck. Here's what a typical box contains:

黒豆 kuromame
Black soybeans boiled with sugar. They are believed to ward off evil spirits, and the word *mame* (bean) also means 'diligent'.

かずのこ kazunoko
Marinated herring roe for fertility and productivity.

田作り tazukuri
Baby sardines simmered nearly dry in soy sauce and sweet sake. *Tazukuri* translates as 'making rice paddies', and symbolises a good harvest.

紅白かまぼこ kōhaku kamaboko
Red and white fishcakes. Red is for warding off evil, and white is for purity.

栗金団 kurikinton
Chestnuts covered with golden cream usually made from sweet potato. Chestnuts, or *kachiguri* (かち栗) are associated with the verb *katsu* (勝つ), which means 'to win', and the golden colour for richness.

ぶりのやきもの buri no yakimono
Grilled amberjack. This fish has different names in Japanese as it grows, so it is eaten in the hope of development or promotion.

えびのやきもの ebi no yakimono

Grilled shrimp. Shrimp is a symbol of longevity because of its long antennae and curved shape – to symbolise remaining active even when your posture is bent.

紅白なます kōhaku namasu

Shredded radish and carrot marinated in vinegar. The red and white of the vegetables are for good luck.

昆布巻き kobumaki

Simmered sea kelp rolled with fish meat or burdock. Konbu (昆布), meaning 'kelp', is a pun on *yorokobu* (喜ぶ), or 'to rejoice'. The rolled shape refers to books, and this dish is for academic achievement.

八つ頭 yatsugashira

Simmered taro is for fertility, as root vegetables produce plenty of crops.

March: Girl's Day

Hinamatsuri (ひな祭り), or Girl's Day, is when we hope for and celebrate the healthy growth of girls in our families.

On 3rd March, we put out decorations and dolls depicting a scene from courtly life in the Heian period. The dolls of a prince and his consort are placed on the top of a decorative display, with their ladies-in-waiting and courtly musicians in the lower parts, together with elaborately made miniatures of furniture and ox-drawn carts, creating scenes of the domestic bliss of elegant, well-to-do families of a bygone era.

As a boy, I had little interest in a celebration using dolls. My interests were mostly to do with the treats served. There is *amazake* (甘酒), a sweet, mostly non-alcoholic *sake*, and sweet rice cakes called *hishimochi* (菱餅).

The popular myth is that the longer the display is left out past Girl's Day, the harder it will be for the girls of such households to get married. From playing house to this unwarranted pressure to marry from a very early age, I am not sure if this festival can withstand modern-day scrutiny.

April: cherry blossom and back to school

Just as the English talk endlessly about the weather, the Japanese talk incessantly about the changing seasons.

Appreciating cherry blossom *en masse* for its beauty alone is a relatively recent phenomenon, dating back to the Edo period, when city dwellers had become the cultural force. The flowering of the cherry blossom coincides with the end and beginning of the Japanese academic year.

There is talk of aligning the Japanese academic year with the rest of the world to start in autumn and ending in summer. Apart from the ease of transferring between overseas and domestic education systems, a more serious argument is that it would be better not to leave kids unattended for a month and a half of summer holiday after only three months of the new school year. While the arguments for change have some force, it is unlikely to happen. The Japanese are too attached to having the cherry blossom as a backdrop to the beginning of new chapters in their lives.

May: Boy's Day

The day for celebrating boys and wishing for their healthy growth is on 5th May.

On Boy's Day we take out miniature armour, swords and arrows for display, representing a family's wish for their boys to grow up to be brave and strong. *Yoroi kabuto* (鎧兜) means armour, and boys' hearts soar at the sight of an awesome martial display. Inevitably, the miniature swords are the first to get damaged from too much mock fighting.

If a family has the space and equipment, they may hoist *koinobori* (鯉のぼり), which are windsocks made to look like carp. From the ancient Chinese myth, carp are believed to swim upstream to a source, and those reaching riverheads turn into dragons. Hence, it is a symbol of future success.

Boy's Day treats are usually *kashiwamochi* (柏餅), rice cakes wrapped in oak leaves. As oak leaves do not fall until new shoots appear, they symbolise unbroken family lineage. This is a tradition borrowed from a Chinese festival commemorating the death of poet Qu Yuan.

June: the rainy season

Japan's geographic location exposes it to East Asian monsoons. At the beginning of every summer, warm air over the Pacific Ocean pushes back relatively cold air above the Asian continent, creating a weather front that brings rain.

While rain is not a pleasant weather phenomenon, especially when accompanied with the rising humidity and temperature of an oceanic climate, the Japanese have long appreciated the benefits that the seasonal rain brings. *Megumi no ame* (恵みの雨) is our term for the 'benevolence of rain'.

The fresh water supply of Japan's river systems relies on two sources and one key factor. One source is winter snowfall, and the other is seasonal rain. The key factor is the ability of mountains to soak it up and act as natural reservoirs. Due to our population explosion, Japan has built many reservoir dams in the mountains at considerable cost, both financial and environmental. Whether or not more are needed is a topic for heated political debate, both locally and nationally.

July: the summer holidays

As explained, the Japanese school year begins in April, while the summer holidays usually start in the middle of July. Therefore, teachers, especially in primary schools, usually pile homework and assignments on children to be done during the holiday.

Although their lives may be hijacked by PlayStation and Xbox, a child's typical summer holiday would feature at least some of the following:

Swimming pools: Schools have pools, and open them to the public during the holidays. This prompts children to go back to school voluntarily, but just to exhaust themselves splashing about and to catch up with their friends.

A visit to the beach: As an island nation, Japan has no shortage of seaside, and no summer family outing is complete without at least one visit to the beach. Usually, the game of suikawari (スイカ割り) is played, in which a blindfolded player attempts to find and crack open a suika, or watermelon, by hitting it with a stick while the spectators try to navigate the player. Even if you know where the watermelon is, you are not supposed to hit it with too much force and crush it to smithereens – cool and juicy watermelon is one of summer's unmissable delights.

A visit to the mountains: There is relatively cool air during the summer in the peaks, especially compared to the concrete jungle below. The mountains are also heaven for children who have a fascination with insects. Apart from ever-annoying mosquitos, there are colourful butterflies to be observed and noisy cicadas to be caught. The king of them all is the beetle. Especially valued are kabutomushi (カブトムシ – rhinoceros beetles), with their unicorn-like horn, and kuwagata mushi (クワガタムシ – stag beetles), with antler-like pincer jaws. These beetles have become so popular that there are people running businesses of growing and selling them at a high price.

August: Obon

August is the height of summer in Japan. The sun beats down mercilessly, and the asphalt roads feel like frying pans. People move slowly if forced to go outside. They tend to lock themselves up at home with air-con watching high-school baseball on TV.

It is also the month of *Obon* (お盆), the Japanese version of what is known in China as the 'Hungry Ghost Festival'. It comes from the Buddhist parable about the sorrow of one of Buddha's followers for his deceased parents, who are suffering in their afterlives as *gaki* (餓鬼), or eternally hungry ghosts. To ease his conscience, Buddha told the man that the ghosts would be permitted to return home for a limited period and that he could take care of them during that time to ease their suffering. The tradition came to Japan with the introduction of Buddhism, then mingled with its indigenous ancestral worship to become *Obon*. Celebrated on 15th August, *Obon* is a family affair, and people tend to return to their ancestral homes for this occasion.

In my family, my late grandmother made a big fuss of the festival. She cleaned the family *butsudan* (仏壇), or Buddhist altar, especially for the occasion, and decorated it with fresh flowers and special lanterns. Then she told us children to go to the temple where our family cemetery was, with a handheld lantern and unlit candles. At the cemetery, we were to summon the ancestral spirits and light a candle in the lantern, even in the bright daylight of the August sun. It was supposed to light the way back home for the spirits, she said. Arriving at home, grandmother did an amazing piece of play-acting, welcoming each of the ancestors she had known personally by addressing them each in turn. The spirits stayed at home for three nights and four days, sharing mealtimes with the living (a small set of dishes were served at the family altar). On the fourth day, we led the spirits to the bank of a riverside, or any waterway, and saw them off back to the afterlife by making a little bonfire. This was, of course, the climax of my grandmother's performance, saying her goodbyes to all the spirits, presumably floating downriver to the world of the dead.

A lighter form of entertainment during *Obon* period is *bonodori* (盆踊り), or an *Obon* dance party. Each local community builds a makeshift platform in a public space, and people dance around it after sundown to traditional Japanese music, usually clad in *yukata*, the type of *kimono* made with thin cotton cloth.

September–November:
autumn harvest festivals

The Japanese word for autumn is *aki* (秋). It is said that the word comes from *akiru*, which means 'getting tired of', because people wished for a harvest so abundant that they would get tired of too much food.

Once the crops are harvested, it is time to celebrate. Throughout Japan, there are festivals held in local shrines, with a focus on giving thanks to the gods for a good harvest, or, in the case of bad years, praying for a better harvest in the next year.

Shinto festivals usually feature the parading of *mikoshi* (神輿), or a portable altar. These are attached to two planks and are meant to be carried around on peoples' shoulders. The average *mikoshi* weighs about 500kg (there are some weighing over a ton). Shrines usually have their own societies of *mikoshi*-bearers who, at festival time, don the traditional attire of *happi* (法被), or *hanten* (半纏), both types of a short, jacket-style kimono, and walk about the neighbourhood with their *mikoshi* on their shoulders with much gusto.

Autumn is also the season when people start being active again after the unbearable summer heatwave. There are slogans such as 'Autumn is for Sports' or 'Autumn for Arts', encouraging people to engage in activities. By far the most popular slogan is 'Autumn is for Healthy Appetite', encouraging people to gorge on the fruits of the harvest.

Autumn is also for indulging in another typically Japanese activity of enjoying the changing seasons. In a custom called *momijigari* (紅葉狩り), or 'hunting for autumn colours', people go outdoors to appreciate the changing leaves on the trees. While it isn't as boisterous as the hunt for the spring cherry blossom, the mountains nevertheless are filled with people in search of visual treats. Famous spots like Karasawa in Nagano prefecture see large 'villages' of tent-dwellers springing up to take part in this outdoor visual feast.

THE LITTLE BOOK OF JAPANESE LIVING

December: the end of the year

In old Japanese, December was called *shiwasu* (師走) meaning that the masters were running about being busy.

Today December is also a busy month. The business world tries to get as much done as possible before the year-end, as little is achieved with the New Year holiday mood in January, and then you are only the short month of February away from the end of the fiscal year in March. December is not a good month for business trips to Japan.

Christmas Eve on the 24th is somehow regarded as romantic in Japan, like most of the newly imported Western customs are. Young couples are expected to go on dates and cheeky restaurants hike their prices for the day.

The 30th is called *misoka* (晦日), or the 'last day of the month' – a custom dating back to the days of the lunar calendar, where each month usually consisted of 30 days. Offices usually close on or before the 30th, and each workplace holds what is called *shigoto osame* (仕事納め), or 'closing of work', perhaps with a little speech from the boss and exchanges of good wishes among the colleagues for the new year.

The 31st is known as *Ōmisoka* (大晦日), or the 'great last day of the month', because it is also the end of the year. People are back at home, busy with preparations to welcome in the coming year, cooking traditional New Year's dishes, and carrying out *ōsōji* (大掃除), or the 'grand cleaning', to get rid of the bad luck of the past year and to welcome in good luck for the new year.

Towards midnight, all the Buddhist temples throughout Japan start banging their gongs 108 times. The number 108 represents the number of cares that each person carries in his or her life in accordance with Buddhist teaching. With each toll of the gong, people are expected to let go of their cares and be ready for the New Year.

Brimming with creative inspiration, how-to projects and useful information to enrich your everyday life, Quarto Knows is a favourite destination for those pursuing their interests and passions. Visit our site and dig deeper with our books into your area of interest: Quarto Creates, Quarto Cooks, Quarto Homes, Quarto Lives, Quarto Drives, Quarto Explores, Quarto Gifts, or Quarto Kids.

First published in 2018 as *How to Live Japanese* by White Lion Publishing, an imprint of The Quarto Group.
The Old Brewery, 6 Blundell Street,
London, N7 9BH,
United Kingdom
T (0)20 7700 6700 F (0)20 7700 8066
www.QuartoKnows.com

This edition first published in 2020 by White Lion Publishing

A catalogue record for this book is available from the British Library.

UK ISBN 978 0 71124 992 9
US ISBN 978 0 7112 5350 6
Ebook ISBN 978 0 71124 993 6

10 9 8 7 6 5 4 3 2 1

Design by Ginny Zeal
Illustrations by Taku Bannai
Photography by Shohki Eno

All photography courtesy of Shohki Eno with the following exceptions:
p.122l ©Studio Ghibli, courtesy of Everett Collection/Alamy
p.122r ©Studio Ghibli, courtesy of Photo 12 / Alamy Stock Photo
p.137 & 139 ©YSK1Shutterstock

Shohki would like thank the following people and locations for their help with the project:
p.36-7 Location: Tenonji, 天恩山五百羅漢寺
p.115 Location: Igo salon TENGEN Shinjyuku, 囲碁サロン 天元 新宿